The Bigger Picture:

Visions of the Future

Alles Digitale zu diesem Buch kann auf der Lernplattform **allango** von Ernst Klett Sprachen abgerufen werden. So geht's:

QR-Code scannen oder **www.allango.net** aufrufen | Buchtitel oder ISBN in der Suche eingeben und auf das Buchcover klicken | Zum Inhalt navigieren, direkt abrufen oder speichern

Visions of the Future

Herausgegeben
von Sarah Garman

Ernst Klett Sprachen
Stuttgart

Bildquellenverzeichnis:
stock.adobe.com, Dublin: Cover; **S.6** (fotos4people); Cover; **S. 6** (Edelweiss); Cover; **S. 6** (psdesign1); Cover; **S. 6; S. 162** (BrunoWeltmann); Cover; **S. 6; S. 11** (Innovated Captures); Cover; **S. 6; S. 161** (Mopic); Cover; **S. 6; S. 12** (Picture-Factory); Cover; **S. 6; S. 60** (Sergey); Cover; **S. 6; S. 59** (sdecoret)

1. Auflage 4 | 2025

Alle Drucke dieser Auflage sind unverändert und können im Unterricht nebeneinander verwendet werden.
Die letzte Zahl bezeichnet das Jahr des Druckes.
www.klett-sprachen.de

Herausgeberin: Sarah Garman
Redaktion: Paul Newcomb
Layoutkonzeption: Greta Gröttrup
Gestaltung und Satz: bostext, 71292 Friolzheim
Umschlaggestaltung: Greta Gröttrup
Druck und Bindung: Elanders Waiblingen GmbH, Waiblingen

Printed in Germany
ISBN 978-3-12-580010-6

Contents

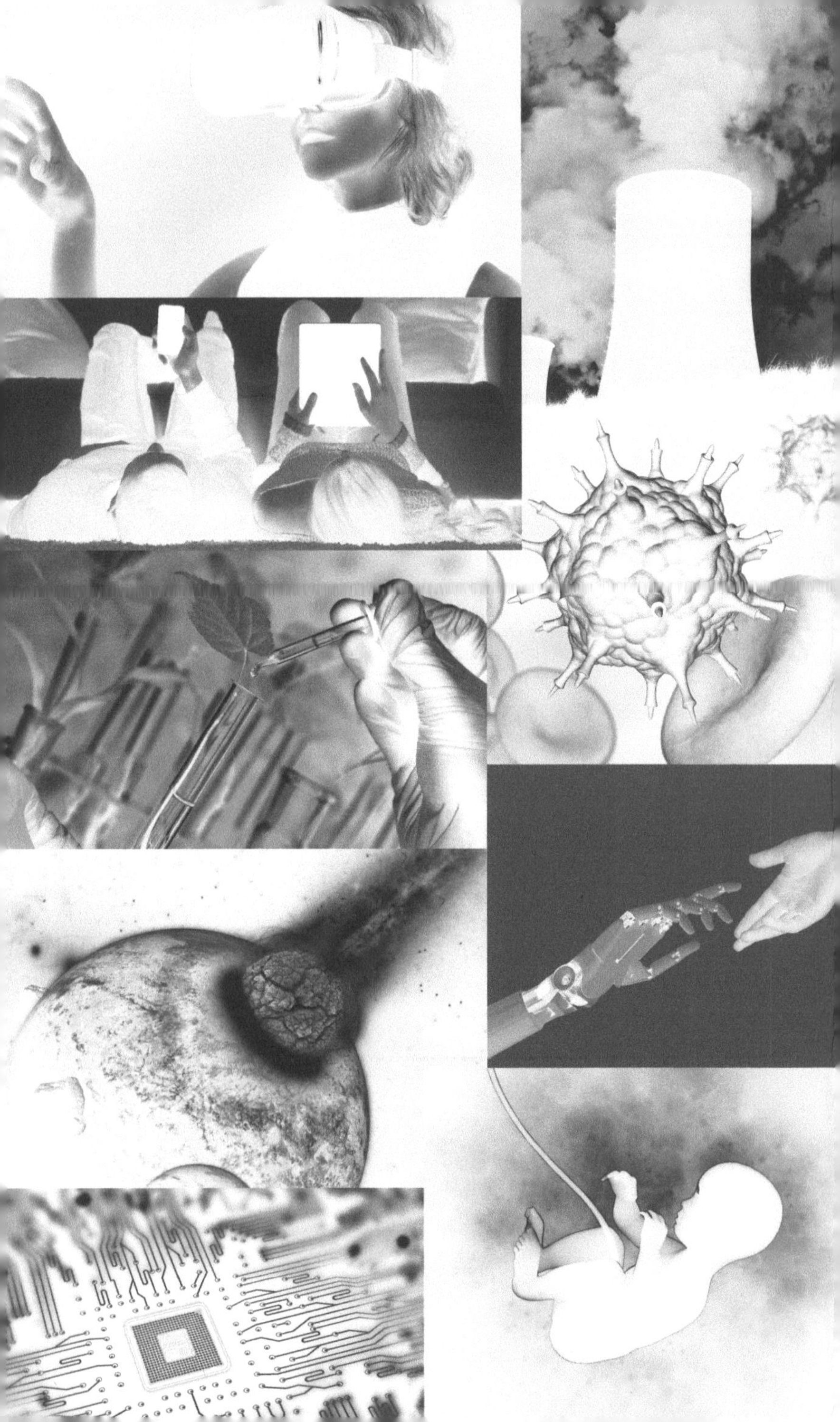

The Bigger Picture

The Bigger Picture is a series of books and further materials in English which deals with a selection of topical, social, literary and political issues of modern life, and which should help you to form a bigger picture of the world we live in.

Each theme-based collection consists firstly of a series of challenging and motivating shorter texts, in various formats – mostly short stories, extracts from popular novels or longer, in-depth feature articles taken from major national newspapers.

Each Student's Book has its own tailor-made Teacher's Guide, full of further ideas and tasks suitable for learning in groups and individual learners.

To make the scope of the series as broad and interesting as possible, carefully selected materials in a multi-media, multi-channel approach consisting of:

- **the texts in the Student's book**
- **relevant sound files**
- **motivating video and**
- **extensive internet links to further reading**

are moulded together to help *you* form *your* "Bigger Picture".

Learning about the world and its issues is motivating in itself. Plus, of course, being able to understand more by reading and listening, as well as of course actively talking and writing about them in English, will help you shine with knowledge and competence when you do your English *Abi*!

Online material

The contents of this book refer, in various places, to additional material – an audio file, pictures, videos, a PDF file and links to further articles of interest. This is always indicated in the text.

You can access these materials in two ways. The first option is: go to *www.klett-sprachen.de* and enter a code into the search field:

For materials and links in **Section 1** (How are our lives changing in a "post-factual" world?), use online-link yu64kqw.

For Section 2 (Dystopian literature: The genre): yww53kb.

For Section 3 (Medical ethics): fpcyxaw.

The second option is: go to *allango* (see p. 1)

Visions of the Future

For as long as people have been conscious (and consciousness is one definition of our species – what makes us different from other living creatures), we have always had "Visions of the Future".

We have come a long way since the dawn of civilization, and throughout this time people everywhere have lived in constant change – social, economic, technological, medical. The fact that change is constant makes us wonder sometimes how things might be in future. We ask ourselves which inventions will enhance our possibilities, opportunities – and risks. We wonder which changes will affect us, and how? How can we shape the world so it is more pleasurable for us all to live in? How might things go wrong?

Of course, we cannot see into the future, but this only makes the speculation more fascinating.

This collection of texts is divided into three basic areas.

Firstly we pose the question: "How are our lives changing now?"

Then Section 2 deals with dystopian literature from historical, technological and political perspectives.

Section 3 rounds things off with an ethically based exploration of selected aspects of advances in medicine.

We hope that you enjoy getting "the bigger picture", and will feel inspired to seek and understand your own Visions of the Future.

Abbreviations used in this book

abb abbreviation
adj adjective
adv adverb
AE American English
BE British English
coll colloquial
derog derogatory
e.g. for example
esp especially
fig figurative
fml formal
hum humorous
idm idiom
i.e. that is
inf informal
Lat Latin
mus music
n noun
off offensive
old old-fashioned
opp opposite
pl plural
sb somebody
sl slang (be careful how you use it!)
sth something
usu usually

1 How are our lives changing?

Introduction

How often do you use social media? How many hours a week do you spend "googling" things you want to know or need for school? When you want to meet up with friends, do you call or send them a message on WhatsApp, or use some other medium?

With the incredible advancements in technology and the boom of the World Wide Web, our lives have changed drastically. No longer must we spend hours at the library researching for school papers, just "Google" it. And why wait by the phone for your friend to call you back, just send her a message on WhatsApp. Want to share the best pictures from your holiday with your family? No need to print them out, just post them online – to Facebook, perhaps?

These developments and apps bring us closer together, not only with our family and friends, but also with people around the world. However, there are some disadvantages to this concept of instant sharing and easily available information. Google, for instance, is a powerful tool for research and finding answers to questions you can't ask anyone else. But everything you type into the Google search engine is collected, to study human behavior. Whatsapp, the free messaging app, is a multi-billion dollar company … but where does the money come from? What do they do with the data about ourselves that we feed into it?

And while Facebook allows you to stay connected to friends, it also is a site where you can become someone completely new.

The texts in this section will look more closely at these ideas and challenge you, as a reader, to reflect critically on this technological age we live in.

Tasks

1. **Have you ever seen something online that didn't seem to be true? An article or maybe even a fake profile? Be prepared to share the experience with a partner.**

2. **Define the word "transparency" in this context. How could your definition relate to your use of technology and social media?**

Text 1: Cancer cons, phoney accidents and fake deaths: meet the internet hoax buster

by Rachel Monroe

After Taryn Wright exposed an elaborate fake tragedy on Facebook, she found herself leading a squad of online detectives – but on the internet, it doesn't take long for a crowd to become a mob.

On 13 May 2012, friends of Dana Dirr, a 35-year-old surgeon in Saskatchewan, were greeted with a distressing message when they logged into Facebook: "URGENT PRAYERS NEEDED." A post written by Dirr's father informed her friends that Dana was fighting for her life after a head-on car accident. Dana had been airlifted to the very same trauma centre where she worked as a surgeon; in fact, she was meant to be on duty that night. "Dana is almost 35 weeks pregnant now," her father wrote. "So please pray for her and the baby!"

Within hours, hundreds of people had shared the post of Dana's accident, and hundreds more had left supportive comments. As she fought for her life, her family continued to post updates to Facebook. Minutely detailing their lives online was nothing new for the Dirrs. Dana's husband, a tattooed ex-punk named JS, had been active in online communities for at least a decade – and had acquired hundreds of online-only friends (and at least one online lover). In 2010, Dana and JS had even become minor internet celebrities when they began sharing the story of their seven-year-old son Eli, who was in the midst of his fourth battle with cancer, with a growing

2 **to expose** [ek'spoʊz] *(inf)* to reveal, show *(enthüllen)* – 3 **squad** [skwɑ:d] group with a leader *usu* in a military context – 6 **Saskatchewan** [səs'ketʃəwən] province in Canada – 10 **trauma centre** hospital specializing in major injuries – 10 **surgeon** doctor who performs medical operations – 19 **to acquire** [ə'kwaɪɚ] to gain – 23 **in the midst of** in the middle of sth

number of followers – first a few hundred, then a few thousand. They called him Warrior Eli.

Friends of the Dirrs returned to their Facebook page for the rest of the day in search of new updates. Late that night, JS announced that baby Evelyn was delivered healthy at 11.11pm; shortly afterwards, at 12.02am, Dana died. Her husband saw this timing as Dana's final act of courage: "She wouldn't have wanted Evie's birthday to be overshadowed by her death every year," he wrote. "She waited until just two minutes after midnight on Mother's Day to leave us."

The family's friends and followers asked about setting up a crowdfunding campaign to provide financial support during this time of trouble, but JS demurred. The Canadian healthcare system would be footing the bills, he said. Instead, the family asked for donations to be made to Alex's Lemonade Stand, a childhood cancer charity.

Those who had got to know the Dirrs online mourned Dana's death. "I spent my night before Mother's Day in tears and every time I told my story yesterday I was in tears on Mothers Day!!" one Facebook friend wrote later – she also donated $50 to Alex's Lemonade Stand.

In a cosy house in the southern suburbs of Chicago, Taryn Wright watched the dramatic saga of Dana Dirr's death unfold online in real time. Wright was in her early 30s and was living with her parents at the time, practically immobile after major hip surgery. She dealt with the depressing lack of autonomy and mobility as best she could – mostly by knitting and "doing paint-by-numbers like a serial killer".

---

7 **courage** *Mut* – 8 **to overshadow** to cast a shadow over sth, to seem more important than sth, sb – 12 **crowdfunding campaign** a site people can donate money to so that sth can be achieved, e.g. a charity – 14 **to foot the bill** to pay for the expenses – 23 **saga** ['sɑːɡə] a long eventful story *usu* with a hero – 26 **autonomy** freedom, independence

When Wright stumbled upon the ostentatiously tragic story of Dana Dirr, she quickly came to feel that something did not add up. Dana's dramatic death and the birth of her baby – on Mother's Day, no less – was not being reported anywhere in the media. And the more Wright looked into it, the more the entire Dirr family saga, chronicled in a decade's-worth of blogposts, MySpace pages, and online photo albums, did not ring true, either. There were too many kids, and too many of them were twins. There were murders and mistaken identities and dramatic ironies. It all sounded suspiciously like a soap opera.

Wright took a few of the hundreds of family photos that the Dirrs had posted online and plugged them into a reverse image search, which allows users to see where else an image has appeared on the internet. She found that the photographs had been lifted from a South African blogger. What's more, Dana Dirr was supposedly a trauma surgeon, but there was no profile for her on a hospital's website, or any search result that had not been written by one of the Dirrs themselves.

Wright felt increasingly certain that Dana Dirr did not exist. The discovery both incensed and invigorated her. Her first instinct was to tell all the people whose photos had been stolen about the hoax. But instead of emailing each one of them, she decided to create a blog to announce her suspicions. She called it 🔗 Warrior Eli Hoax Group.

A link made the rounds on Facebook, and within hours a group of like-minded sceptics began gravitating to the blog, posting their own findings in the comments section. Some had been Facebook

---

1 **ostentatiously** *(adv)* in an extreme way and meant to impress – 6 **to chronicle** ['krɑ:nikl] to record detailed events as they happen – 14 **lifted** taken, stolen – 20 **incensed** extremely angry – 20 **invigorated** filled with energy and purpose – 21 **hoax** [həʊks] an elaborate fake story – 23 🔗 **For online link, use code yu64kqw at klett-sprachen.de. For Klett Augmented, scan page 11.** – 26 **sceptics** *(pl)* people who question the truthfulness of stories

friends with the Dirrs and were shocked to find they had been duped; some were caregivers who were active in the childhood cancer community, outraged by the deception; and others, like Wright, had no personal connection but were drawn to the oddness of the whole situation.

After having figured out that Dana Dirr probably did not exist, Wright started looking into Dirr's Facebook friends. "When I Googled their names, nothing came up," she recalled. "And when I started looking up their photos, I found that they had been stolen, too." Not only did Dana Dirr not exist, Wright determined, but neither did her husband or her sick son. More than 70 of the Dirrs's Facebook friends were fake, too.

Wright, a dark-haired woman with precisely arched eyebrows, has long been drawn to stories of serial killers, serial liars, and cult leaders. (A few years ago, she and her sister pledged to stop bringing up the Jonestown mass suicide on first dates.) She had obsessively followed the twisted stories of several women who had been caught creating elaborate fake personas online in the early days of the internet. There was Kaycee Nicole, a teenager dying of leukaemia who turned out to be a healthy middle-aged woman. And Jesse Jubilee James, a cowboy-fireman-poet with suicidal tendencies and liver cancer, who was actually the creation of a woman in her mid-50s. Now Wright found herself in the heady position of being the detective, uncovering a hoax of her own.

"At the beginning, it felt like a giant puzzle to solve," Wright said. She also started a Facebook group to facilitate the investigation; in the span of an hour, a hundred people joined to help her sift through online clues. Unnerved and exhilarated, Wright closed the group to new members. She stayed up all night, drinking Diet Coke

---

2 **duped** [du:pt] fooled, deceived – 26 **to facilitate** to make efforts or processes easier – 27 **to sift (through)** to search

and refreshing the site to check for new comments as the puzzle pieces came together. In less than a day, her makeshift blog got 100,000 hits. It was the first hint that what Wright had started might get beyond her control.

■

In 1951, the British endocrinologist Richard Asher identified a class of patients who presented dramatic symptoms and told fantastic stories of illness and woe. When credulity and sympathy began to wear thin in one town, they simply moved down the road and began again with a new set of doctors, nurses and neighbours. Asher called this illness Munchausen syndrome.

Munchausen patients pose a problem for clinicians, in that their sickness involves pretending to be sick. Sometimes that pretending blurs the line between "real" and "fake" illness: Munchausen patients have been known to bleed themselves in order to appear anaemic, or to dose themselves with chemotherapy drugs they don't need.

Several years ago, after noticing an increase in similar behaviour online, 🔗 **Dr Marc Feldman**, a clinical professor of psychiatry at the University of Alabama, coined the term 🔗 "**Munchausen by internet**" to describe people who spread accounts of fake illness online. "For most of these deceivers, sympathy and attention is the main thing," Feldman told me. "They get nurturance they feel unable to get in any other way. They may have poor social skills or poor coping strategies, and pretending to be ill allows them to manifest this instant and caring community.

---

6 **endocrinologist** doctor who treats hormone-based diseases – 8 **woe** sorrow, sadness – 12 **clinician** medical worker who sees patients – 15 **anaemic** [əˈniːmɪk] *(adj)* suffering from a disease in which the patient is pale and sickly because he or she has a lack of red blood cells – 18 🔗 **For online link, use code yu64kqw at klett-sprachen.de. For Klett Augmented, scan page 11.** – 19 🔗 **For online link, use code yu64kqw at klett-sprachen.de. For Klett Augmented, scan page 11.** – 22 **nurturance** *(n)* care, love – 24 **coping strategies** ways to deal with bad situations or problems

"Before the advent of the internet, people would have to read medical textbooks or go to medical libraries to learn about esoteric ailments," said Feldman. "They had to practise their pain faces in the mirror, then go to the ER and enact a painful crisis of some sort for the staff. Now you can go to Wikipedia and become an expert on an ailment in 20 minutes. Then you go online and instantly find a supportive community."

When people from that supportive community realise that their sympathy (and sometimes money) has been extracted under false pretences, they may, like victims of financial fraud, feel too ashamed to talk about it. Others – such as those who flocked to the Warrior Eli Hoax blog – take it one step further, turning their embarrassment into revenge, becoming online vigilantes.

In May 2012, Wright wrote dozens of blogposts about the Dirrs. She traced a photo of Dana Dirr's pregnant belly back to a New York mother, and tracked down 10-year-old blogposts about the tragic murder of JS's (fictional) twin. As the updates rolled in, the site's audience kept growing. Wright found herself in the centre of an odd, passionate group of amateur online detectives. Her hundred-strong Warrior Eli Hoax Facebook group made researching the Dirr case easier. One person would share expertise on a rare form of childhood cancer, while another would turn out to know about tracking down IP addresses.

It did not take long for the group to figure out who was behind the Dirr drama. Several of the family's supporters had received packages of plastic bracelets with a message of support for Warrior Eli. The packages had been sent and paid for by JS's sister, Emily. Unlike the other Dirr family members, Emily Dirr did have an online presence; she was a medical student in Ohio. Wright was

---

2 **esoteric ailments** rare illnesses – 9 **extracted** taken – 13 **vigilante** [ˌvɪdʒɪˈlænti] sb who tries to get justice or revenge, but not through the police or legal methods

convinced that she had enough information to publicly out Emily, but she wanted to speak to the hoaxer first. In a phone conversation that Wright recalls as "surreal," Emily admitted in a quiet monotone that she had created the whole saga. The story, which she had begun in 2004, was a way to keep herself entertained, like fan fiction about a group of characters of her own invention.

"This all started 11 years ago when I was a bored 11-year-old kid looking for an escape from the pain and heartache I saw in my own family," Emily Dirr wrote in a public apology posted on Wright's website. "It started almost as fiction writing, but the more time I spent escaping to it, the more 'real' it became. I am so sorry it hurt so many real families, and so many people out there."

Hearing this, some group members were out for blood. They wanted the young woman prosecuted – for fraud, for impersonating someone else, for whatever they could get her for.

One of the loudest and angriest voices in the Warrior Eli Hoax group was an odd character named Father James Puryear. According to Puryear's Facebook profile, he was a 16-year-old single father who hoped to become a preacher. He was the one who found the Dirrs' old Photobucket account, which had turned out to be an important clue. He also professed to be shocked and horrified that anyone would pretend to be someone else online. But in the group's first week, when members started introducing themselves, "he posted this long, insane thing", Wright recalls. "'I was raped when I was this age. Then I had a kidnapping, and then my twin did this.' Just like every kind of red flag." Her suspicions aroused, Wright asked for photos of Puryear's two kids. Puryear sent a photo of a kid wearing a Halloween mask. Wright said she did not believe the photographs were real and Puryear did not send any more. Wright

3 **surreal** [sə'ri:l] a mix of fantasy and reality – 14 **to prosecute** *strafrechtlich verfolgen* – 14 **to impersonate sb** to pretend to be another specific person – 21 **to profess** to proclaim, to tell in front of many people

booted Puryear out of the group. Barely two weeks later, Father James Puryear – who turned out to be a 24-year-old Massachusetts woman named 🔗 Carissa Hads – was arrested in West Virginia. Hads later pleaded guilty to posing as Puryear in order to have sex with a 15-year-old girl she had been talking to over the internet for more than a year.

After that, Wright made sure to verify group member's real identities. But the idealism of those first few weeks was shattered. "It made me think about, like, who are these people that I'm sharing stuff with in here? Because it felt great at first – we were all great friends," Wright says, and sighs. "I'm too trusting."

■

For some people, cancer has acquired a strange allure. In John Green's blockbuster young adult novel *The Fault in Our Stars*, tragic, beautiful young people with terminal diagnoses are alternately funny and profound as they face their fates. Online, some cancer victims have even become celebrities. Since the early days of the internet, patients and their families have shared their stories online as a way to cope with the isolating effects of illness. There are hundreds of these pages on the internet, most of them genuine, the great majority on Facebook – Prayers for Shane, 🔗 Hope for Hannah, Rally for Rowan. Many of these groups originated as a way to communicate with friends, family, and colleagues, but it does not take long for strangers to start tuning in, too. The most popular cancer blogs have tens of thousands of followers. They fundraise

3 🔗 **For online link, use code yu64kqw at klett-sprachen.de. For Klett Augmented, scan page 11.** – 7 **to verify** to make certain sth is true – 13 **allure** [e'lʊr] appeal, attraction – 15 **terminal** deadly, no cure – 20 **genuine** real, honest – 21 🔗 **For online link, use code yu64kqw at klett-sprachen.de. For Klett Augmented, scan page 11.** – 22 **to originate** to begin

by selling T-shirts and bumper stickers, and their stories sometimes become famous enough to merit articles in mainstream magazines.

This attention has inspired people eager for the privileged status of the sick – the sympathy, if not the suffering, of real cancer patients and their "courageous battles". "The heroic image that cancer survivors increasingly have is attractive to factitious disorder patients," Marc Feldman writes in his scholarly book *Playing Sick.*

In September 2012, Taylor Swift wrote a song dedicated to Ronan Thompson, a three-year-old boy who died of neuroblastoma, featuring lyrics taken from 🔗 **Ronan's mother's popular blog**. After Swift's song was released on iTunes, dozens of blogs by mothers with dying children started popping up – many of them actually written by Swift-obsessed high-school students hoping to get their idol's attention with a tragic story of their own. (The Warrior Eli Hoax team investigated many of these blogs, though they generally did not publicly post information about teenage hoaxers.)

By the summer of 2012, Wright's inbox was filling up with emails reporting potential hoaxers. She shared the details with the Facebook group, which began investigating them as well. Diana Almanza, a stay-at-home mother in North Carolina, joined the group because she wanted to see how the Emily Dirr story turned out. "When someone sends you something that they think is fake, it's very hard not to do something," she told me. "You can't look away. It gets under your skin, I guess."

As the months ticked by, the hundred-odd members of the Warrior Eli Hoax group honed their detective skills. They investigated a part-time rodeo rider with leukaemia; a terminally ill 21-year-old;

2 **to merit** to deserve, to be worth sth – 10 **neuroblastoma** cancer that forms early on in nerve cells of a fetus – 11 🔗 **For online link, use code yu64kqw at klett-sprachen.de. For Klett Augmented, scan page 11.** – 27 **to hone sth** [hoʊn] to make sth perfect – 28 **rodeo** cattle-herding and bull-riding sport

and an amnesiac teenager undergoing "extreme chemotherapy"; each one was exposed as a fake. Some hoaxers hid behind made-up names and stolen photos; others posted under their own names and seemed to be faking cancer in real life, too.

Some of the hoaxes were pathetic – the woman who posed as a dying (male) soccer player online stole photos of David Beckham for her fake Facebook profile – but others were extensive and elaborate. Hoaxers shaved their heads and bought medical equipment on the internet to make their hospital selfies look more realistic. Many of these hoaxers were fooling lots of people. One had even been voted "patient of the year" by the US Leukemia & Lymphoma Society; another had used crowdfunding websites to raise thousands of dollars.

The detectives had learned to spot telltale signs – alleged cancer patients who were bald, but still had their eyebrow hair; sick people supposedly on steroids who didn't have the typical puffy-faced appearance. Exposing a hoaxer sometimes took more than 100 hours of research, poring over potential fakers' Facebook pages and trying to connect a name with an IP address. "We always want to be 1,000 % sure," said Almanza.

■

In January 2013, Taryn Wright invited a few dozen friends and family over to her house for a party. The occasion was an episode of the American news programme 20/20 about online hoaxers that featured the Dirr case and an interview with Wright, her first appearance on TV. Wright was relieved after watching the segment with her interview; it seemed to go well. Then the programme

---

7 **extensive** in depth, very long – 14 **alleged** [əˈledʒɪd] supposed *(angeblich)* – 26 **relieved** no longer anxious

showed something Wright had not expected – hidden camera footage of hoaxer Emily Dirr walking down the street. She looked frumpy and exhausted, about as far as you could get from JS Dirr, her swaggering online alter ego, with his tattoos and twins and many lovers. Wright's friends and relatives laughed and pointed.

Wright felt sick. "She was just walking down the street eating a candy bar." Wright says. "And everybody is laughing, saying, 'Look at her, she looks like a troll. She's probably always eating a candy bar.' But I'm thinking, She probably worked hard to get the pieces of her life together and all of a sudden she's on Channel 7 on a Friday night, and everyone is laughing at her. What if it had been me? That would be horrible."

After the show aired, Wright became increasingly uncomfortable about the responsibility she was taking on by inserting herself into people's lives. That autumn, the group researched a young woman whose Tumblr detailed her long battle with cancer – and who was collecting money with a GoFundMe page. Her stories turned out to have been largely stolen from a legitimate cancer blogger. The group had figured out the name of the person behind the hoax and its members were close to building a convincing case against her when the woman announced on her Tumblr that she was going to kill herself.

The more Wright chatted with hoaxers, the more she felt convinced that they were suffering from mental illness.

From her research, Wright knew that the woman lived in Florida with her brother. When she started announcing concrete, specific plans, Wright decided she had to call the police. "Hi, I'm Taryn, and I live in Chicago," she told the police dispatcher, unsure whether they would dismiss her as some kook from the internet. She was

---

3 **frumpy** *(adj)* looking unclean, wearing oversized clothes – 24 **convinced** *(adj)* certain, sure (of sth) – 29 **kook** *(sl)* crazy person

pleased when they took her report seriously. After the holidays, Wright contacted the woman's brother to check up on her. He said that she had been taken in for treatment on Christmas Eve; to Wright, this felt like a victory. (Since then, she has reported at least three other possibly suicidal hoaxers to police.)

Wright also spent hours talking to hoax victims. "I'd out people, and then I'd feel responsible. I wanted to make sure everyone was OK. I didn't feel like I could ignore emails from people who were angry or grieving. So I ended up talking on the phone a bunch after each case," she says. She even formed phone friendships with some of the hoaxers themselves, including a young woman in California named Jadzia, who had faked several pregnancies and one bout of cancer.

The more time Wright spent chatting with hoaxers, the more she felt convinced that they were suffering from mental illness. "If someone is looking at their own life and thinking, 'I would rather write about living the life of somebody who's dying,' something's going on there. I don't think that they're well. I don't think that a happy person goes and does this," Wright says. She learned to recognise the typical hoaxer profile: a socially isolated woman in her early 20s, often "a little chunky", sometimes depressed. Wright, who has had her own struggles with weight and depression, saw a more desperate version of herself in some of these women.

Because Wright is the public face of the hoax-exposing world, many people friended her on Facebook – including hoax victims, fellow detectives, and sometimes even the hoaxers themselves. Having all those people together in the same virtual room got contentious at times. "Jadzia will like a photo I posted, and then other people will question me about it – 'Is that the Jadzia you wrote about on your blog?' And it's just like, 'Yeah, you know, we're

---

21 **chunky** *(sl)* overweight – 28 **contentious** controversial (it started arguments)

friends,'" Wright says. "They've done bad things, but I have a lot of friends who've done bad things, and it's not like I'm going to walk away from them. I guess it's a little weird because I've met them because they did bad things. But the way I see it, that's only one side of it."

■

I met Wright last summer at her parents' house in the southern suburbs of Chicago. That day, she was looking into a woman who posted online as Diabetic Gymnast, and who had suffered an improbable number of tragedies – multiple cancers, an abusive stepfather, rape, a rare blood disease – in her 20-year-life. Wright skimmed the Diabetic Gymnast's stories of blood test results and suicide attempts with narrowed eyes. Something in her seemed to quicken when she turned up a potential clue: a reference to a specific hospital, a photograph that didn't look quite right.

Wright is sharp and self-deprecating, two qualities that come across strongly in her internet writing. She is also obsessive, with a precise recall for all the minute details of the cases she has worked on. Listening to her, I sometimes found myself lost amid all the overblown and oddly repetitive drama: "Wait, *whose* twin was that? Was the adoption real or fake?

People drawn to online sleuthing are a particular bunch, by turns noble and self-righteous, obsessed with justice and occasionally fanatical. Their interest in tragedies that do not directly relate to their lives – at least until they put themselves in the middle of them – can sometimes seem propelled by empathy, and other times by

---

8 **suburbs** a group of neighborhoods *usu* where there are many family homes *(Vorstadtviertel)* – 10 **improbable** unlikely – 16 **self-deprecating** modest in a humorous way – 22 **sleuthing** ['slu:θɪŋ] looking for clues, acting like a detective

prurience. Inevitably, such online communities often hit by their own little cyclones of infighting and drama.

But for its first year of existence, it seemed as though the Warrior Eli Hoax group was different. After the strange incident with Father James Puryear/Carissa Hads, there were no fights or scandals. Wright did not even have to moderate the comments. But over time, that began to change. The tone of the comments became angrier: "I want to punch her in the throat," one group member wrote about a hoaxer. "I have nothing but contempt and disgust for her as a human being," wrote another. (Both of those commenters had lost close family members to cancer, Wright points out.)

Wright started hearing from people who were mentioned on the blog – not just the hoaxers, but their friends or family members, people who were only tangential characters in one of the cases. It turned out that her blog's readers were contacting them via Facebook, sometimes angrily and other times just out of curiosity. "People feel like they are entitled to the true story behind things, and don't see these stories as involving real people," said Wright. "It's like everybody is the TV journalist who comes in with a camera and says, 'How do you feel about your kid getting hit by a car?'"

Around the same time, things began deteriorating among the core group of detectives in the **Warrior Eli Hoax Facebook group**. If Wright voiced sympathy for a hoaxer, other group members would post dozens of incensed replies. "There was more and more of the 'Let's lynch her' mentality [when the group identified a hoaxer]. I began to feel weird about posting personal stuff about other people in the big group because I wanted to make sure that the people who were helping investigate were on the same page that

1 **prurience** being obsessed by sexual activity – 14 **tangential** indirectly related – 22 **For online link, use code yu64kqw at klett-sprachen.de. For Klett Augmented, scan page 11.**

I was: that we were doing an educational thing, trying to help people get better – not a vengeance thing," she said.

Talking about the unravelling of the Facebook group is clearly painful for Wright. She considered many of her fellow detectives to be friends. Most of them, she insisted, are good people. "I understand why they got upset. They saw their own child go through leukaemia, and lose their hair, and die. So for them, somebody faking that and taking a child's pictures who died of cancer and saying that this is their child, that hits them in a different way than it hits me. So I don't feel like I could tell them, 'Don't feel like this,'" she said. "At the same time, I don't want to feel like that."

■

The kindness of strangers has helped families pay for treatment, raised money for research and provided support in dark times. But, through her hoax-exposing work, Wright has also seen how the online cancer community can sometimes become vicious. As Wright became increasingly well-known online, she began to receive messages asking her to investigate parents. Many of these emails mentioned one woman in particular, who frequently posted on charity websites requesting video games for her special needs son, Jayden. "I got emails about her, maybe 10 a day, saying look into this, look into that," Wright recalled.

Wright has herself become a target for abuse. One day last year, she received an unexpected and unwelcome piece of mail.

But the problem was that Jayden's mother was not a hoaxer. "Their concern wasn't the legitimacy," said Wright. Instead, Jayden's mother's critics accused her of asking for too many video games,

---

2 **vengeance** seeking revenge – 16 **vicious** [ˈvɪʃəs] extremely mean

and she had responded to their snide comments by lashing out. Such tantrums are deviant behaviour in a community that is all about gratitude, heart emojis and inspirational quotations about hope.

The conflict unsettled Wright. The community simply seemed not to like Jayden's mother and had turned on her. "If the parent doesn't mind their Ps and Qs 100%, or is kind of a hillbilly and gets into screaming matches online, they'll start Facebook groups like, Ban Hope for Jayden," explained Wright. "Or they'll Google this woman and find out she'd been arrested in the 90s for something, and anytime she posts an update on her legitimately sick child, somebody will link to the arrest report from back to 1991. It's crazy."

Wright has herself become a target for abuse. In April 2013, she received an unexpected and unwelcome piece of mail: a certified letter from a lawyer threatening a lawsuit for defamation for her posts about a cancer faker named Chelsea Hassinger. But when she took a closer look, something about the letter seemed off. It looked as though it had been printed out on a regular piece of computer paper. "It wasn't, like, attorney paper," she says. She Googled the name of the law firm and got no hits. But when she called the phone number listed on the letterhead, the voicemail informed her that she had reached the law firm of Gorman and Rickman. If it was a trick or a scam, it was certainly an elaborate one.

The more Wright looked into it, the more she was convinced it was fake. Still, she was spooked. The person behind it clearly wanted her to feel intimidated – and they knew her home address. Not long after, Wright discovered the blogs: The Truth About Taryn Wright, Taryn Wright Is Wrong, among others. Whoever was behind these

1 **to lash out** to hit or kick at sb, in this case with words – 2 **deviant** abnormal – 7 **mind their P's and Q's** *(idm)* to choose their words carefully; be very polite – 7 **hillbilly** *(AE sl, off)* person who lives away from society, *usu* uneducated

blogs had included unflattering photos from Wright's deleted weight loss blog and private information about her sister. The vengeful blogger even sent Facebook messages to all of Wright's friends, accusing her of being a liar.

The campaign of harassment lasted about four months before petering out. Wright says that the same person – a hoaxer's angry friend – was behind the blogs and the fake lawyer's letter but declines to say more for fear of inspiring more antagonism. But the experience clearly rattled her. "I knew that there would be stuff that came out about me, and I was willing to take that risk," she says. "But don't post stuff about my sisters. Don't post stuff about people who I care about."

As she dealt with the cancer community's Mean Girl clique – the vengeance-seeking detectives, her online stalker, the distraught hoax victims calling her up at all hours – hoax-hunting was all starting to feel so much more messy than it had at the start. As she told me these stories, I imagined the hoaxers and the hoax-hunters both online late at night, the blue light of their computer screens casting an eerie glow on their faces as they immersed themselves in lives that were not their own.

In June 2013, Wright removed everyone from the Warrior Eli Facebook group except for four other people, including Diana Almanza. The remaining members are all dedicated posters with solid research skills, and, most importantly, they are all in agreement about how to handle hoaxers. These days, the group generally opts to research and resolve a case without posting it to the blog. Only particularly egregious hoaxes make it to the blog.

"We don't want [hoaxers] villainised," says Almanza. "They have a mental illness. They certainly do bad things, and there are times

---

5 **harassment** repeated mistreatment – 25 **to opt** to choose – 27 **egregious** [ɪˈgriːdʒəs] incredibly shocking

you research and you get really angry with them. But, my hope for all them is that, by being exposed and helping to get them treatment, they can move on and have happier, more productive lives."

Wright has not worked full-time since the blog took off. She has applied for plenty of jobs, but whenever she gets close there is a moment when her prospective boss gets a pained look and says something like, "So, we Googled you ..."

I asked Wright if she ever regrets her impulsive decision to start the blog that day in May, 2012. "I don't know," she said, after a long pause. "I'm proud of what I did. I think that I went into it with good intentions. I think that I have continued with good intentions. I've met some great people, people that will be my friends for ever." But at the same time, her own experiences of harassment have made her empathise with the hoaxers she has exposed. "[The harassment] felt like such a violation to me – how does it feel like to the people I write about? A lot of people have told me that it's a totally different thing, because I'm not doing anything wrong. But at the same time, it's the same feeling. And I don't like the feeling."
(5,085 words)

Text 2: Extract from *The Circle* (2013)

by Dave Eggers

In The Circle, a best-selling novel first published in the USA in 2013, Mae, a recent college graduate, is a new employee for the worldwide tech company called The Circle, which is run by three "wise men" – Eamon Bailey, Ty, and Stenton. She begins working in customer service, answering calls and solving problems while being integrated into campus life and the culture of the company.

In her first few weeks, she meets the mysterious Kalden, with whom she begins an affair. Then, at a company gathering, the new SeeChange camera is presented – a portable camera which allows for real-time transmission of everything a person sees and does at all times – and the promise of transparency is used to pressure politicians, and eventually everyone, into wearing the cameras.

At this point in the novel, Bailey is interviewing Mae in front of the Circle employees about an experience she had which she did not share with anyone…

---

12 **to pressure sb into doing sth** to force sb to do sth; to make sb do sth (*usu* against their will)

"Hello, Circlers," he said.

"Hello Eamon!" they roared back.

"Thank you for being here today, on a very special Dream Friday. I thought we'd change it up a bit today and have not a speech, but an interview. As some of you know, we do these from time to time to shed light on members of the Circle and their thoughts, their hopes, and in this case, their evolutions."

He sat in one of the chairs and smiled into the wings. "I had a conversation with a young Circler the other day that I wanted to share with you. So I've asked Mae Holland, who some of you might know as one of our newbies in Customer Experience, to join me today. Mae?"

Mae stepped into the light. The feeling was of instant weightlessness, of floating in black space, with two distant but bright suns blinding her. She couldn't see anyone in the audience, and could barely orient herself to the stage. But she managed to direct her body, her legs made of straw, her feet leaden, toward Bailey. She found her chair, and with two hands, feeling numb and blind, lowered herself into it.

"Hello Mae. How are you?"

"Terrified."

The audience laughed.

"Don't be nervous," Bailey said, smiling to the audience and giving her the slightest look of concern.

"Easy for you to say," she said, and there was laughter throughout the room. This laughter felt good and calmed her. She breathed in, and looked in the front row, finding five or six shadowy faces, all smiling. She was, she realized and now felt in her bones, among friends. She was safe. She took a sip of water, felt it cool everything inside her, and put her hands in her lap. She felt ready.

---

6 **to shed light on sb** to reveal sth about sb – 11 **newby** *(pl:* **newbies***) (sl, inf)* new person (in a company, etc) – 17 **leaden** ['ledən] made of lead *(bleiern)*

"Mae, in one word how would you describe the awakening you had this past week?"

This part they had rehearsed. She knew Bailey wanted to start with this idea of an awakening. "It was just that, Eamon"—she'd been instructed to call him Eamon—"it was an awakening."

"Oops. I guess I just stole your thunder," he said. The audience laughed. "I should have said, 'What did you have this week?' But tell us, why that word?"

"Well, 'awakening' seems right to me ..." Mae said, and then added " ... now."

The word "now" appeared a split-second later than it should have, and Bailey's eye twitched. "Let's talk about this awakening," he said. "It started on Sunday night. Many of the people in the room already know the broad outlines of the events, with SeeChange and all. But give us a summary."

Mae looked at her hands, in what she realized was a theatrical gesture. She had never before looked at her hands to indicate some level of shame.

"I committed a crime, basically," she said. "I borrowed a kayak without the knowledge of the owner, and I paddled to an island in the middle of the bay."

"That was Blue Island, I understand?"

"It was."

"And did you tell anyone you were doing this?"

"No, I didn't."

"Now Mae, did you have the intention of telling anyone about this trip afterward?"

"No."

"And did you document it at all? Pictures, video?"

"No, nothing."

---

6 **to steal sb's thunder** *(idm)* to say sth which spoils the surprise that they wanted to cause – 14 **SeeChange** see the Introduction to this extract

There were some murmurs from the audience. Mae and Eamon had expected a reaction to this revelation, and they both paused to allow the crowd to assimilate this information.

"Did you know you were doing something wrong, in borrowing this kayak without the owner's knowledge?"

"I did."

"But you did it anyway. Why?"

"Because I thought no one would know."

Another low murmur from the audience.

"So this is an interesting point. The very fact that you thought this action would remain secret enabled you to commit this crime, correct?"

"Correct."

"Would you have done it had you known people were watching?"

"Definitely not."

"So in a way, doing all this in darkness, unobserved and unaccountable, it facilitated impulses that you regret?"

"Absolutely. The fact that I thought I was alone, unwatched, enabled me to commit a crime. And I risked my life. I wasn't wearing a life preserver."

Again, a loud murmur rippled through the audience.

"So you not only committed a crime against the owner of this property, but you risked your own life. All because you were being enabled by some, what, some cloak of invisibility?"

The audience rumbled with laughter. Bailey's eyes stayed on Mae, telling her *Things are going well.*

"Right," she said.

---

18 **unaccountable** not answerable; without responsibility – 18 **to facilitate** to make possible – 22 **to ripple** to move like a wave – 25 **cloak of invisibility** coat which you wear and it makes you invisible *(undurchsichtig)*

"I have a question, Mae. Do you behave better or worse when you're being watched?"

"Better. Without a doubt."

"When you're alone, unwatched, unaccountable, what happens?"

"Well, for one thing, I steal kayaks."

The audience laughed in a sudden bright burst.

"Seriously. I do things I don't want to do. I lie."

"The other day, when we spoke, you had a way of putting it that I thought was very interesting and succinct. Can you tell us all what you said?"

"I said that secrets are lies."

"Secrets are lies. It's very memorable. Can you walk us through your logic with that phrase, Mae?"

"Well, when there's something kept secret, two things happen. One is that it makes crimes possible. We behave worse when we're not accountable. That goes without saying. And second, secrets inspire speculation. When we don't know what's being hidden, we guess, we make up answers."

"Well that's interesting, isn't it?" Bailey turned to the audience. "When we can't reach a loved one, we speculate. We panic. We make up stories about where they are or what's happened to them. And if we're feeling ungenerous, or jealous, we make up lies. Sometimes some very damaging lies. We assume they're doing something nefarious. All because we don't know something."

"It's like when we see two people whispering," Mae said. "We worry, we feel insecure, we make up terrible things they might be saying.We assume it's about us and that it's catastrophic."

"When they're probably asking where the bathroom is." Bailey got a big laugh and enjoyed it.

---

10 **succinct** very short and accurate – 25 **nefarious** [nəˈferiːəs] bad, criminal

"Right," Mae said. She knew she was approaching a few phrases she needed to get right. She'd said them in Bailey's library, and she just needed to say them again the way she'd first said them. "For example, if there's a locked door, I start to make up all kinds of stories about what might be behind it. I feel like it's some kind of secret and it leads to me making up lies. But if all the doors are open, physically and metaphorically, there's only the one truth."

Bailey smiled. She'd nailed it.

"I like that, Mae. When the doors are open, there's only one truth. So let's recap that first statement of Mae's. Can we get that on the screen?"

The words SECRETS ARE LIES appeared on the screen behind Mae. Seeing the words four feet tall gave her a complicated feeling—something between thrill and dread. Bailey was all smiles, shaking his head, admiring the words.

"Okay, we've resolved that had you known that you'd be held accountable for your actions, you wouldn't have committed this crime. Your access to the shadows, in this case illusory shadows, facilitates bad behavior. And when you know you're being watched, you are your better self. Correct?"

"Correct."

"Now let's talk about the second revelation you made after this episode. You mentioned that you didn't document this trip to Blue Island in any way. Why not?"

"Well, first of all, I knew I was doing something illegal."

"Sure. But you've said that you often kayak in the bay, and you'd never documented these trips. You hadn't joined any Circle clubs devoted to kayaking, and you hadn't posted accounts, photos, video,

---

8 **to nail it** *(idm)* to get sth perfectly right – 10 **recap** to repeat – 22 **revelation** *Enthüllung*

or comments. Have you been doing these kayak trips under the auspices of the CIA?"

Mae, and the audience, laughed. "No."

"Then why these secret trips? You haven't told anyone about them before or after, you haven't mentioned them anywhere. No accounts exist of any of these excursions, am I right?"

"You are right."

Mae heard loud clucks spread through the auditorium.

"What did you see on this last trip, Mae? I understand it was quite beautiful."

"It was, Eamon. There was an almost-full moon, and the water was very calm, and I felt like I was paddling through liquid silver."

"Sounds incredible."

"It was."

"Animals? Wildlife?"

"I was followed for a while by a sole harbor seal, and he dipped above and below the surface, as if he was curious, and also urging me on. I'd never been to this island. Very few people have. And once I got to the island, I climbed to the top, and the view from the peak was incredible. I saw the golden lights of the city, and the black foothills toward the Pacific, and even saw a shooting star."

"A shooting star! Lucky you."

"I was very lucky."

"But you didn't take a picture."

"No."

"Not any video."

"No."

"So there's no record of any of this."

"No. Not outside my own memory."

---

2 auspices ['ɑːspɪsɪz] *Schirmherrschaft* – **16 sole** single, lonely, only one

There were audible groans from the audience. Bailey turned to the audience, shaking his head, indulging them.

"Okay," he said, sounding as if he were bracing himself, "now this is where we get into something personal. As you all know, I have a son, Gunner, who was born with CP, cerebral palsy. Though he's living a very full life, and we're trying, always, to improve his opportunities, he is confined to a wheelchair. He can't walk. He can't run. He can't go kayaking. So what does he do if he wants to experience something like this? Well, he watches video. He looks at pictures. Much of his experiences of the world come through the experiences of others. And of course so many of you Circlers have been so generous, providing him with video and photos of your own travels. When he experiences the SeeChange view of a Circler climbing Mount Kenya, he feels like he's climbed Mount Kenya. When he sees firsthand video from an America's Cup crew member, Gunner feels, in some way, that he's sailed in the America's Cup, too. These experiences were facilitated by generous humans who have shared what they saw with the world, my son included. And we can only extrapolate how many others there are out there like Gunner. Maybe they're disabled. Maybe they're elderly, homebound. Maybe a thousand things. But the point is that there are millions of people who can't see what you saw, Mae. Does it feel right to have deprived them of seeing what you saw?"

Mae's throat was dry and she tried not to show her emotion. "It doesn't. It feels very wrong." Mae thought of Bailey's son Gunner, and thought of her own father.

"Do you think they have a right to see things like you saw?"

"I do."

---

5 **cerebral palsy** *Zerebralparese* – 19 **to extrapolate** to guess – 22 **to deprive sb of doing sth** to stop sb from doing sth

"In this short life," Bailey said, "why shouldn't everyone see whatever it is they want to see? Why shouldn't everyone have equal access to the sights of the world? The knowledge of the world? All the experiences available in this world?"

Mae's voice was just above a whisper. "Everyone should."

"But this experience you had, you kept it to yourself. Which is curious, because you do share online. You work at the Circle. Your PartiRank is in the T2K. So why do you think this particular hobby of yours, these extraordinary explorations, why hide these from the world?"

"I can't quite figure out what I was thinking, to be honest," Mae said.

The crowd murmured. Bailey nodded.

"Okay. We just talked about how we, as humans, hide what we're ashamed of. We do something illegal, or unethical, and we hide it from the world because we know it's wrong. But hiding something glorious, a wonderful trip on the water, the moonlight coming down, a shooting star …"

"It was just selfish, Eamon. It was selfish and nothing more. The same way a child doesn't want to share her favorite toy. I understand that secrecy is part of, well, an aberrant behavior system. It comes from a bad place, not a place of light and generosity. And when you deprive your friends, or someone like your son Gunner, of experiences like I had, you're basically stealing from them. You're depriving them of something they have a right to. Knowledge is a basic human right. Equal access to all possible human experiences is a basic human right."

Mae surprised herself with her eloquence, and the audience answered with thunderous applause. Bailey was looking at her like

21 **aberrant** mistaken, wrong – 28 **eloquence** high ability with words and speaking to an audience

a proud father. When the applause subsided, Bailey spoke softly, as if reluctant to get in her way.

"You had a way of putting it that I'd like you to repeat."

"Well, it's embarrassing, but I said that sharing is caring."

The audience laughed. Bailey smiled warmly.

"I don't think it's embarrassing. This expression has been around for a while, but it applies here, doesn't it, Mae? Maybe uniquely apropos."

"I think it's simple. If you care about your fellow human beings, you share what you know with them. You share what you see. You give them anything you can. If you care about their plight, their suffering, their curiosity, their right to learn and know anything the world contains, you share with them. You share what you have and what you see and what you know. To me, the logic there is undeniable."

The audience cheered, and while they did so, three new words, Sharing Is Caring, appeared on the screen, below the previous three. Bailey was shaking his head, amazed.

"I love that. Mae, you have a way with words. And there's one more statement you made that I think should cap off what I think everyone here would agree has been a wonderfully enlightening and inspiring talk."

The audience clapped warmly.

"We were talking about what you saw as the impulse to keep things to yourself."

"Well, it's not something I'm proud of, and I don't think it rises above the level of simple selfishness. Now I really understand that. I understand that we're obligated, as humans, to share what we see and know. And that all knowledge must be democratically accessible."

---

11 plight [plaɪt] bad situation

"It's the natural state of information to be free."

"Right."

"We all have a right to know everything we can. We all collectively own the accumulated knowledge of the world."

"Right," Mae said. "So what happens if I deprive anyone or everyone of something I know? Aren't I stealing from my fellow humans?"

"Indeed," Bailey said, nodding earnestly. Mae looked to the audience, and saw the entire first row, the only faces visible, nodding, too.

"And given your way with words, Mae, I wonder if you can tell us this third and last revelation you made. What did you say?"

"Well, I said, privacy is theft."

Bailey turned to the audience. "Isn't that an interesting way of putting it, guys? 'Privacy is theft.' " The words now appeared on the screen behind him, in great white letters:

PRIVACY IS THEFT

Mae turned to look at the three lines together. She blinked back tears, seeing it all there. Had she really thought of all that herself?

SECRETS ARE LIES
SHARING IS CARING
PRIVACY IS THEFT

Mae's throat was tight, dry. She knew she couldn't speak, so she hoped Bailey wouldn't ask her to. As if sensing how she felt, that she was overcome, he winked at her and turned to the audience.

"Let's thank Mae for her candor, her brilliance, and her consummate humanity, can we please?"

---

26 **candor** openness, honesty – 27 **consummate** perfect

The audience was on its feet. Mae's face was on fire. She didn't know if she should sit or stand. She stood briefly, then felt silly, so sat down again, and waved from her lap.

Somewhere in the stampeding applause, Bailey managed to announce the capper to it all—that Mae, in the interest of sharing all she saw and could offer the world, would be going transparent immediately.

[...]

[BOOK II]

It was a bizarre creature, ghostlike, vaguely menacing and never still, but no one who stood before it could look away. Mae was hypnotized by it, its slashing form, its fins like blades, its milky skin and wool-grey eyes. It was certainly a shark, it had its distinctive shape, its malevolent stare, but this was a new species, omnivorous and blind. Stenton had brought it back from his trip to the Marianas Trench, in the Circle submersible. The shark was not the only discovery—Stenton had retrieved heretofore unknown jellyfishes, seahorses, manta rays, all of them near-translucent, ethereal in their movements, all on display in a series of enormous aquariums he'd had constructed, nearly overnight, to house them.

Mae's tasks were to show her watchers the beasts, to explain when necessary, and to be, through the lens worn around her neck, a window into this new world, and the world, generally, of the Circle. Every morning Mae put on a necklace, much like Stewart's, but lighter, smaller, and with the lens worn over her heart. There, it presented the steadiest view, and the widest. It saw everything that Mae saw, and often more. The quality of the raw video was such that viewers could zoom, pan, freeze and enhance. The audio was

---

4 **stampeding** *here*: very enthusiastic, loud – 9 **menacing** ['menəsɪŋ] threatening – 11 **fin** *Flosse* – 12 **malevolent** [mə'levələnt] threatening, evil – 13 **omnivorous** eating everything – 16 **heretofore** [ˌhɪrtu:fɔr] up until now – 17 **ethereal** very light, delicate and graceful

carefully engineered to focus on her immediate conversations, to record but make secondary any ambient sound or background voices. In essence, it meant that any room she was in was scannable by anyone watching; they could focus in on any corner, and, with some effort, isolate and listen to any other conversation.

There was to be a feeding for all of Stenton's discoveries any minute, but the animal she and her watchers were particularly interested in was the shark. She hadn't yet seen it eat, but word was it was insatiable and very quick. Though blind, it found its meals immediately, no matter how big or small, alive or dead, and digested them with alarming speed. One minute a herring or squid would be dropped into the tank with it, and moments later the shark would deposit, on the aquarium floor, all that remained of that animal—a tiny grainy substance that looked like ash. This act was made more fascinating given the shark's translucent skin, which allowed an unfettered view into its digestive process.

She heard a droplet through her earpiece. "Feeding moved back to 1:02," a voice said. It was now 12:51.

Mae looked down the dark hallway, to the three other aquariums, each of them slightly smaller than the one before it. The hall was kept entirely unlit, to best highlight the electric-blue aquariums and the fog-white creatures within.

"Let's move over to the octopus for now," the voice said.

The main audio feed, from Additional Guidance to Mae, was provided via a tiny earpiece, and this allowed the AG team to give her occasional directions—to suggest she drop by the Machine Age, for example, to show her watchers a new, solar-powered consumer drone that could travel unlimited distances, across continents and seas, provided adequate exposure to sun; she'd done that visit earlier

---

8 **word was…** it was said that… – 9 **insatiable** [ɪnˈseɪʃəbᵊl] *(adj) unersättlich* – 14 **grainy** powder-like – 15 **translucent** [trænzˈluːsənt] transparent

this day. This was a good portion of her day, the touring of various departments, the introduction of new products, either Circle-made or Circle-endorsed. It ensured that every day was different, and had, in the six weeks she'd been transparent, exposed Mae to virtually every corner of the campus—from the Age of Sail to the Old Kingdom, where they were, on a lark more than anything, working on a project to attach a camera to every remaining polar bear.

"Let's see the octopus," Mae said to her viewers.

She moved over to a round glass structure sixteen feet high and twelve feet in diameter. Inside, a pale spineless being, the hue of a cloud but veined in blue and green, was feeling around, guessing and flailing, like a near-blind man fumbling for his glasses.

"This is a relative of the telescope octopus," Mae said, "but this one has never been captured alive before."

Its shape seemed to change continuously, balloon-like and bulbous one moment, as if inflating itself, confident and growing, then the next it would be shrinking, spinning, stretching and reaching, unsure of its true form.

"As you can see, its true size is very hard to discern. One second it seems like you could hold it in your hand, and the next it encompasses most of the tank."

The creature's tentacles seemed to want to know everything: the shape of the glass, the topography of the coral below, the feel of the water all around.

"He's almost endearing," Mae said, watching the octopus reach from wall to wall, spreading itself like a net. Something about its curiosity gave it a sentient presence, full of doubt and wanting.

"Stenton found this one first," she said about the octopus, which was now rising from the floor, slowly, flamboyantly. "It came from

---

6 **on a lark** for fun – 10 **spineless** *(adj) wirbellos* – 10 **hue** [hjuː] color; appearance – 16 **bulbous** very circular, fat – 21 **to encompass** here: to fill – 25 **endearing** likable *(sympathisch)* – 27 **sentient** capable of feeling – 29 **flamboyantly** extravagantly

behind his submersible and shot in front, as if it were asking him to follow. You can see how fast it might have moved." The octopus was now careening around the aquarium, propelling itself in motions like the opening and closing of an umbrella.

Mae checked the time. It was 12:54. She had a few minutes to kill. She kept her lens on the octopus.

She was under no illusion that every minute of every day was equally scintillating to her watchers. In the weeks Mae had been transparent, there had been downtime, a good deal of it, but her task, primarily, was to provide an open window into life at the Circle, the sublime and the banal. "Here we are in the gym," she might say, showing viewers the health club for the first time. "People are running and sweating and devising ways to check each other out without getting caught." Then, an hour later, she might be eating lunch, casually and without commentary, across from other Circlers, all of them behaving, or attempting to, as if no one was watching at all. Most of her fellow Circlers were happy to be on-camera, and after a few days all Circlers knew that it was a part of their job at the Circle, and an elemental part of the Circle, period. If they were to be a company espousing transparency, and the global and unending advantages of open access, they needed to be living that ideal, always and everywhere, and especially on campus.

Thankfully, there was enough to illuminate and celebrate within the Circle gates. The fall and winter had brought the inevitable, all of it, with blitzkrieg speed. All over campus there were signs that hinted at imminent Completion. The messages were cryptic, meant to pique curiosity and discussion. *What would Completion mean?* Staffers were asked to contemplate this, submit answers, and write on the idea boards. *Everyone on Earth has a Circle account!* one

---

8 **scintillating** [ˈsɪnt̬ᵊleɪt̬ɪŋ] sparkling, exciting – 19 **period** *(AE)* full stop, i.e. that is the end of the discussion here – 20 **to espouse** to claim; say that sth is very important – 27 **to pique** [pi:k] to stimulate

popular message said. *The Circle solves world hunger*, said another. *The Circle helps me find my ancestors*, said yet another. *No data, human or numerical or emotional or historical, is ever lost again*. That one had been written and signed by Bailey himself. The most popular was *The Circle helps me find myself*.

So many of these developments had been long in the planning stages at the Circle, but the timing had never been quite so right, and the momentum was too strong to be resisted. Now, with 90 percent of Washington transparent, and the remaining 10 percent wilting under the suspicion of their colleagues and constituents, the question beat down on them like an angry sun: what are you hiding? The plan was that most Circlers would be transparent within the year, but for the time being, to work out the bugs and get everyone used to the idea, it was just Mae and Stewart, but his experiment had been largely eclipsed by Mae's. Mae was young, and moved far quicker than Stewart, and had her voice—watchers loved it, comparing it to music, calling it like woodwind and a wonderful acoustic strum—and Mae was loving it, too, feeling daily the affection of millions flow through her.

It took getting used to, though, starting with the basic working of the equipment. The camera was light, and after a few days, Mae could barely sense the weight of the lens, no heavier than a locket, over her breastbone. They'd tried various ways to keep it on her chest, including velcro attached to her clothing, but nothing was as effective, and simple, as simply hanging it around her neck. The second adjustment, one she found continually fascinating and occasionally jarring, was seeing—through a small frame on her right wrist—what the camera was seeing. She'd all but forgotten

---

8 **momentum** unstoppable gravitational forwards force – 10 **to wilt** to fade; become weaker – 17 **woodwind** *Holzblasinstrument* – 18 **strum** *Anschlag, z.B. bei einer Gitarre* – 19 **affection** friendliness; mild form of love – 24 **velcro** *Klettverschluss* – 27 **jarring** *(adj) schrill*

about her left-wrist health monitor, but the camera had made essential the use of this, a second, right-wrist bracelet. It was the same size and material as her left, but with a larger screen to accommodate video and a summation of all of her data on her usual screens. With a bracelet on each wrist, each snug and with a brushed-metal finish, she felt like Wonder Woman and knew something of her power—though the idea was too ridiculous to tell anyone about.

On her left wrist, she saw her heartbeat; on her right, she could see what her watchers were seeing—a real-time view from her lens, which allowed her to make any necessary adjustments to the view. It also gave her current watcher numbers, her rankings and ratings, and highlighted the most recent and most popular comments from viewers. At that moment, standing before the octopus, Mae had 441,762 watchers, which was a little above her average, but still less than what she'd hoped for while revealing Stenton's deep-sea discoveries. The other numbers displayed were unsurprising. She was averaging 845,029 unique visitors to her live footage in any given day, and had 2.1 million followers to her Zing feed. She no longer had to worry about staying in the T2K; her visibility, and the immense power of her audience, guaranteed stratospheric Conversion Rates and Retail Raws, and ensured she was always in the top ten.

"Let's see the seahorses," Mae said, and moved to the next aquarium. There, amid a pastel bouquet of coral and flowing fronds of blue seaweed, she saw hundreds, maybe thousands, of tiny beings, no bigger than the fingers of a child, hiding in nooks, clinging to the foliage. "Not particularly friendly fish, these guys. Wait, are they even fish?" she asked, and looked to her wrist, where a watcher had

19 **Zing feed** The Circle's approximate equivalent to Twitter – 27 **nooks** corners

already sent the answer. *Absolutely a fish! Class Actinopterygii. Same as cod and tuna.*

"Thank you, Susanna Win from Greensboro!" Mae said, and rezinged the information to her followers. "Now let's see if we can find the daddy of all these baby seahorses. As you might know, the male seahorse is the one that carries the offspring. The hundreds of babies you see were birthed just after the daddy arrived here. Now where is he?" Mae walked around the aquarium, and soon found him, about the size of her hand, resting at the bottom of the tank, leaning against the glass. "I think he's hiding," Mae said, "but he doesn't seem to know we're on the other side of the glass here, and can see everything."

She checked her wrist and adjusted the angle of her lens a bit, to get the best look at the fragile fish. He was curled with his back to her, looking exhausted and shy. She put her face, and lens, up to the glass, so close to him she could see the tiny clouds in his intelligent eyes, the unlikely freckles on his delicate snout. He was an improbable creature, a terrible swimmer, built like a Chinese lantern and utterly without defense. Her wrist highlighted a zing with exceptionally high ratings. *The croissant of the animal kingdom*, it said, and Mae repeated it aloud. But despite his fragility, somehow he had already reproduced, had given life to a hundred more like himself, while the octopus and the shark had traced the contours of their tanks and eaten. Not that the seahorse seemed to care. He was apart from his progeny, as if having no clue where they came from, and no interest in what happened to them.

Mae checked the time. 1:02. Additional Guidance spoke through her earpiece: "Shark feeding ready."

---

2 **cod** *Kabeljau* – 13 **lens** *Objektiv* – 17 **improbable** unlikely; unusual – 25 **progeny** offspring *(Nachwuchs)*

"Okay," Mae said, glancing at her wrist. "I'm seeing a bunch of requests that we get back to the shark, and it's after one, so I'm thinking we'll do that." She left the seahorse, who turned to her, briefly, as if not wanting to see her go.

Mae made her way back to the first and largest aquarium, which held Stenton's shark. Above the aquarium, she saw a young woman, with curly black hair and cuffed white jeans, standing atop a sleek red ladder.

"Hello," Mae said to her. "I'm Mae."

The woman seemed ready to say "I know that," but then, as if remembering they were on camera, adopted a studied, performative tone. "Hello Mae, I'm Georgia, and I'll be feeding Mr. Stenton's shark now."

And then, though it was blind, and there was no food yet in the tank, the shark seemed to sense a feast was at hand. It began turning like a cyclone, rising ever-closer to the surface. Mae's watchers had already risen by 42,000.

"*Some*one's hungry," Mae said.

The shark, which had seemed only passingly menacing before, now appeared vicious and wholly sentient, the embodiment of the predatory instinct. Georgia was attempting to look confident, competent, but Mae saw fear and trepidation in her eyes. "Ready down there?" she asked, without taking her eyes off the shark making its way toward her.

"We're ready," Mae said.

"Okay, I'm going to feed the shark something new today. As you know, he's been fed all kinds of stuff, from salmon to herring to jellyfish. He's devoured everything with equal enthusiasm. Yesterday we tried a manta, which we didn't expect him to enjoy, but he didn't

---

7 **sleek** smart; fashionable – 15 **at hand** about to begin – 20 **embodiment** personification – 21 **predatory** *raubtierhaft* – 22 **trepidation** fear

hesitate, and ate with gusto. So today we're again experimenting with a new food. As you can see," she said, and Mae noticed that the bucket she carried was made of lucite, and inside she saw something blue and brown, with too many legs. She heard it ticking against the bucket walls: a lobster. Mae had never thought of sharks eating lobsters, but she couldn't see why they wouldn't.

"Here we have a regular Maine lobster, which we're not sure if this shark is equipped to eat."

Georgia was perhaps trying to put on a good show, but even Mae was nervous about how long she was holding the lobster over the water. *Drop it*, Mae thought to herself. *Please drop it.*

But Georgia was holding it over the water, presumably for the benefit of Mae and her viewers. The shark, meanwhile, had sensed the lobster, had no doubt mapped its shape with whatever sensors it possessed, and was circling quicker, still obedient but at the end of its patience.

"Some sharks can process the shells of crustaceans like this, some can't," Georgia said, now dangling the lobster such that its claw was lazily touching the surface. *Drop it, please*, Mae thought. *Please drop it now.*

"So I'll just drop this little guy into—"

But before she could finish her sentence the shark had risen up and snatched the lobster from the caretaker's hand. By the time Georgia let out a squeal and grabbed her fingers, as if to count them, the shark was already back in the middle of the tank, the lobster engulfed in its jaws, the crustacean's white flesh spraying from the shark's wide mouth.

"Did he get you?" Mae asked.

Georgia shook her head, holding back tears. "Almost." She rubbed her hand as if it had been burned.

---

17 crustaceans *Krustentiere* – **24 squeal** [skwi:l] small scream

The lobster had been consumed, and Mae saw something gruesome and wonderful: the lobster was being processed, inside the shark, in front of her, with lightning speed and incredible clarity. Mae saw the lobster broken into dozens, then hundreds of pieces, in the shark's mouth, then saw those pieces make their way through the shark's gullet, its stomach, its intestines. In minutes the lobster had been reduced to a grainy, particulate substance. The waste left the shark and fell like snow to the aquarium floor.

"Looks like he's still hungry," Georgia said. She was atop the ladder again, but now with a different lucite container. While Mae had been watching the digestion of the lobster, Georgia had retrieved a second meal.

"Is that what I think it is?" Mae asked.

"This is a Pacific sea turtle," Georgia said, holding up the container that held the reptile. It was about as big as Georgia's torso, painted in a patchwork of green and blue and brown, a beautiful animal unable to move in the tight space. Georgia opened the door at one end of the container, as if inviting the turtle to exit if he so chose. He chose to stay where he was.

"There's little chance our shark has encountered one of these, given the difference in their habitats," Georgia said. "This turtle would have no reason to spend time where Stenton's shark dwells, and the shark surely has never seen the light-dappled areas where the turtles live."

Mae wanted to ask if Georgia were truly about to feed that turtle to the shark. Its eyes had beheld the predator below, and was now, with the slow energy it could harness, pushing its way to the back of the container. Feeding this kindly creature to the shark, no matter the necessity or scientific benefit, would not please many of Mae's

---

6 **gullet** *Speiseröhre* – 6 **intestines** [ɪnˈtestɪnz] *Gedärme* – 7 **particulate** *(adj)* made up of small parts – 27 **to harness** [ˈhɑːrnɪs] to bring together; summon up *(aufbringen)*

watchers. Already zings were coming through her wrist. *Please don't kill that turtle. It looks like my granddad!* There was a second thread, though, that insisted the shark, which was not much bigger than the turtle, would not be able to swallow or digest the reptile, with its impenetrable shell. But just when Mae was about to question the imminent feeding, an AG voice came through Mae's earpiece. "Hold tight. Stenton wants to see this happen."

In the tank, the shark was circling again, looking every bit as lean and ravenous as before. The lobster had been nothing to it, a meaningless snack. Now it rose closer to Georgia, knowing the main course was approaching.

"Here we go," Georgia said, and tilted the container until the turtle began sliding, slowly, toward the neon water, which was swirling beneath him—the shark's turning had created a vortex. When the container was vertical, and the turtle's head had cleared the lucite threshold, the shark could wait no longer. It rose up, grabbed the turtle's head in its jaws, and pulled it under. And like the lobster, the turtle was consumed in seconds, but this time it took a shape-shifting that the crustacean hadn't required. The shark seemed to unhook its jaw, doubling the size of its mouth, enabling it to easily subsume the whole of the turtle in one swallow. Georgia was narrating, saying something about how many sharks, when eating turtles, will turn their stomachs inside out, vomiting the shells after digesting the fleshy parts of the reptile. But Stenton's shark had other methods. The shell seemed to dissolve inside the shark's mouth and stomach like a cracker soaked in saliva. And in less than a minute, the turtle, all of it, had been turned to ash. It exited the shark as had the lobster, in flakes that fell ponderously to

9 **ravenous** ['rævənᵊs] very hungry – 14 **vortex** *Wirbel* – 15 **to clear** *here*: to come out of; emerge from – 21 **swallow** *Schluck* – 28 **ponderously** *(adv)* slowly, as though thoughtfully

the aquarium floor, joining, and indistinguishable from, those that had come before.

Mae was watching this when she saw a figure, nearly a silhouette, on the other side of the glass, beyond the aquarium's far wall. His body was just a shadow, his face invisible, but then, for a moment, the light from above reflected on the circling shark's skin, and revealed the figure's face.

It was Kalden.

Mae hadn't seen him in a month, and since her transparency, hadn't heard any word from him. Annie had been in Amsterdam, then China, then Japan, then back to Geneva, and so hadn't had time to focus on Kalden, but the two of them had traded occasional messages about him. How concerned should they be about this unknown man?

But then he'd disappeared.

Now he was standing, looking at her, unmoving.

She wanted to call out, but then worried. Who was he? Would calling to him, capturing him on camera, create some scene? Would he flee? She was still in shock from the shark's digestion of the turtle, from its dull-eyed wrath, and she found she had no voice, no strength to say Kalden's name. So she stared at him, and he stared at her, and she had the thought that if she could catch him on her camera, perhaps she could show this to Annie, and that might lead to some clarity, some identification. But when Mae looked to her wrist, she saw only the darkest form, his face obscured. Perhaps her lens couldn't see him, was watching from a different angle. As she tracked his shape on her wrist, he backed away and walked off into the shadows.

---

8 **Kalden** a mysterious character with whom Mae is having (or was having) an affair –
10 **Annie** Mae's old college friend, who got her the job at The Circle

Meanwhile, Georgia had been nattering about the shark and what they'd witnessed, and Mae hadn't caught any of it. But now she was standing atop her ladder, waving, hoping that Mae was finished, because she had nothing left to feed the animal. The show was over.

"Okay then," Mae said, thankful for the chance to get away and to follow Kalden. She said goodbye and thanks to Georgia, and walked briskly through the dark hallway.

She caught sight of his silhouette leaving through a faraway door, and she picked up her pace, careful not to shake her lens or call out. The door he'd slipped through led to the newsroom, which would be a logical enough place for Mae to be visiting next. "Let's see what's going on in the newsroom," she said, knowing all within would be aware of her approach in the twenty steps it would take her to get there. She also knew that the SeeChange cameras in the hallway, over the doorway, would have caught Kalden, and she'd know sooner or later if it was actually him. Every movement within the Circle was caught on one camera or another, usually three, and reconstructing anyone's movements, after the fact, was only a few minutes' work.

As she approached the newsroom door, Mae thought of Kalden's hands upon her. His hands reaching low, pulling himself into her. She heard the low rumble of his voice. His taste, like some wet fresh fruit. What if she found him? She couldn't take him to the bathroom. Or could she? She would find a way.

She opened the door to the newsroom, a wide space Bailey had modeled on old-time newspaper offices, with a hundred low cubicles, news tickers and clocks everywhere, each desk with a retro analog telephone, a row of white buttons below the numbers, blinking arrhythmically. There were old printers, fax machines, telex

---

1 **nattering** talking about unimportant things, not seriously; chitchat – 10 **picked up her pace** started walking faster – 29 **arrhythmically** [əˈrɪθmikəli] not in a rhythm; in a random way

devices, letterpresses. The decor, of course, was for show. All the retro machines were nonfunctional. The news gatherers, whose faces were now upon Mae, smiling, saying hello to her and her watchers, were able to do most of their reporting via SeeChange. There were now over a hundred million cameras functional and accessible around the world, making in-person reporting unnecessarily expensive and dangerous, to say nothing of the carbon expenditures.

As Mae walked through the newsroom, the staff waved to her, unsure if this was an official visit. Mae waved back, scanning the room, knowing she appeared distracted. Where was Kalden? There was only one other exit, so Mae rushed through the room, nodding and greeting, until she came to the door on the far end. She opened it, flinching at the bright light of day, and saw him. He was crossing the wide green lawn, passing the new sculpture by that Chinese dissident—she remembered she should highlight it soon, maybe even today—and just then he turned briefly, as if checking to see if Mae was still following. Her eyes met his, provoking a tiny smile before he turned again and walked quickly around the Period of Five Dynasties.

"Where are you headed?" the voice in her ear asked.

"Sorry. No place. I was just. Never mind."

Mae was allowed, of course, to go where she pleased—her meanderings were what so many watchers appreciated most—but the Additional Guidance office still liked to check in from time to time. As she stood in the sunlight, Circlers all around, she heard her phone ring. She checked her wrist; there was no caller identified. She knew it could only be Kalden.

"Hello?" she said.

"We have to meet," he said.

---

8 **expenditures** costs – 21 **Where are you headed**? Where are you going? – 24 **meandering** [miˈændərɪŋ] a winding path, *here*: walking around

"Excuse me?" she asked.

"Your watchers can't hear me. They only hear you. Right now your engineers are wondering why the incoming audio isn't working. They'll fix it in a few minutes." His voice was tense, shaky. "So listen. Most of what's happening must stop. I'm serious. The Circle is almost complete and Mae, you have to believe me that this will be bad for you, for me, for humanity. When can we meet? If it has to be in the bathroom that's fine with me—"

Mae hung up.

"Sorry about that," said AG through her earpiece. "Somehow the incoming audio wasn't working. We're working on it. Who was it?"

Mae knew she couldn't lie. She wasn't sure if anyone had indeed heard Kalden. "Some lunatic," Mae improvised, proud of herself. "Babbling about the end of the world."

Mae checked her wrist. Already people were wondering what had happened and how. The most popular zing: *Tech problems at Circle HQ? Next: Santa forgets Christmas?*

"Tell them the truth, as always," AG said.

"Okay, I have no idea what just happened," Mae said aloud. "When I do, I'll let you all know."

But she was shaken. She was still standing, in the sunlight, waving occasionally to Circlers noticing her. She knew her watchers might wonder what was happening next, where she was going. She didn't want to check her wrist, knowing that the comments would be perplexed and even concerned. Off in the distance, she saw what looked like a game of croquet, and alighting on an idea, she made her way to it.

"Now, as you all know," she said when she was close enough to see and wave to the four players, who she realized were two Circlers

---

26 **perplexed** confused, puzzled

and a pair of visitors from Russia, “we do not always play here at the Circle. Sometimes we have to work, which this group is demonstrating. I don’t want to disturb them, but I can assure you that what they’re doing involves problem-solving and complex algorithms and will result in the improving of the products and services we can provide to you. Let’s soak this in.”

That would give her a few minutes to think. Periodically, she would focus her lens on something like this, a game or demonstration or speech, and this might allow her mind to wander, while the watchers watched. She checked the view on her wrist, and saw that her watchers, 432,028, were within the average, and there were no urgent comments, so she permitted herself three minutes before she had to retake control of the feed. With a wide smile—for she was surely visible on three or four outdoor See Changes—she took a breath. This was a new skill she’d acquired, the ability to look, to the outside world, utterly serene and even cheerful, while, in her skull, all was chaos.
(7,486 words)

Tasks

Now you have read the excerpt from “The Circle”, listen to this **interview with Tom Hanks**, who shares his personal views on the story and his character Eamon Bailey in the film of the book. The interview can be accessed via online link yu64kqw or using the Klett Augmented app (scan page 11).

7 **periodically** from time to time – 16 **serene** [sə'ri:n] relaxed – 16 **skull** *Schädel*

Make notes here on what this section has contributed to your bigger picture of "Visions of the Future".

2 Dystopian literature

Introduction: The genre

The word "dystopia" comes from the word "utopia", which is a Greek word which means "no place" or "no-where". A utopia, as written about first in Plato's "Republic", and then by Thomas More in his early 16th Century story, is a perfect place, a place where all social problems have been solved, where goodness prevails and evil has been destroyed. A *dys*topia, on the other hand describes of nightmares, where everything has gone wrong and individuals suffer hardship under an authoritarian regime which caters only for itself and for those that do not rebel.

The idea of dystopian societies has been used by many authors to share their concerns and criticisms of the world. However, each author has a different priority. Some wish to criticize the political system or society in which they live by having futuristic characters discuss "the past", while others attempt to show a potential future if certain changes are not made today. Often, the writer will even set their story on a different planet to show the consequences of humanity's choices.

In order to successfully make people think critically about the main message, authors carefully pick the perspective from which they want the story to be told. Some choose to focus on the political system as a whole, while others center the plot around the struggle of individual characters. This section will take a closer look at three texts that demonstrate these concepts.

Tasks

Pre-Reading tasks: What do you know about it?

1. Create a world which you believe would be perfect. Write a paragraph describing this world.

2. Now watch the short TED Ed video by Alex Gendler: **How to recognize a dystopia**. Be prepared to answer the questions asked at the end.

The interview can be accessed via online link yww53kb or using the Klett Augmented app (scan page 59).

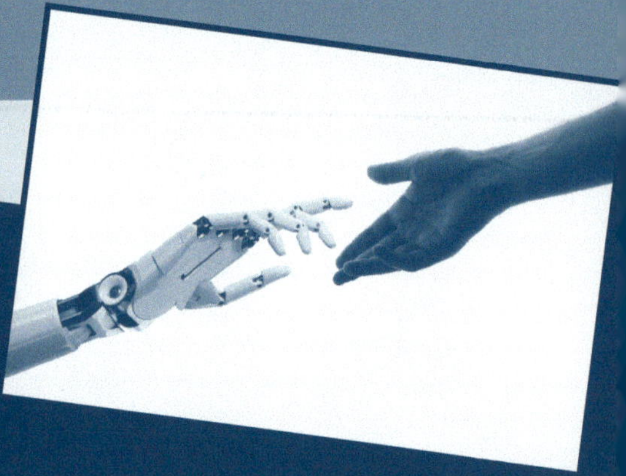

Text 1: The Last American (1889)

by John Ames Mitchell

This story is probably the first piece of literature in any language which is a future history set in a post-apocolyptic world. It thus represents an early landmark in the genre of science-fiction dystopian literature. Written by John Mitchell (1845–1918), it was first published in 1889, six years before H.G. Wells' famous story, "The Time Machine".

The use of names in "The Last American" needs a little explanation. At the time of writing, the field of archaeology was booming with new discoveries. The pyramids by the Nile in Egypt were the main center of archaeological activity, giving rise in this story to the odd looking names, which look Arabic or mid-eastern, but which actually often contain a hidden, often satirical, meaning ("Dimph-Yoo-Chur" is "dim future"; "Kaly-phorn-ya" is "California"). To modern eyes, this may look disrespectful, but 1889 was a very different political environment from today.

"The Last American" is a very good example of a futuristic text which contains criticism of contemporary society. In order to understand this story, we in the early 21st Century need to examine the period and place in which it was written – the USA at the end of the 19th century, a time known in North America as "The Gilded Age".

Tasks

Look at the **illustrations that accompanied the original publication** (access them via online link yww53kb, or by Klett Augmented: scan page 59). Match each one to a gap in the text.

(A **PDF of the original, fully illustrated version** of ***The Last American*** can be accessed the same way – you can check your answers using this version). This activity will familiarize you with the text, and give you a feel for its age and era).

The Last American

A Fragment
from the journal of
KHAN-LI,
PRINCE OF DIMPH-YOO-CHUR AND ADMIRAL IN THE PERSIAN NAVY

Edited by

J.A. MITCHELL

TO
THOSE THOUGHTFUL PERSIANS
WHO CAN READ A WARNING IN THE
SUDDEN RISE AND SWIFT EXTINCTION
OF A FOOLISH PEOPLE
THIS VOLUME IS
DEDICATED

A FEW WORDS BY
HEDFUL,
SURNAMED "THE AXIS OF WISDOM"
Curator of the Imperial Museum at Shiraz. Author of "The Celestial Conquest of Kaly-phorn-ya," and of "Northern Mehrika under the Hy-Bernyan Rulers"

The astounding discoveries of Khan-li of Dimph-yoo-chur have thrown floods of light upon the domestic life of the Mehrikan people. He little realized when he landed upon that sleeping continent what a service he was about to render history, or what enthusiasm his discoveries would arouse among Persian archaeologists.

Every student of antiquity is familiar with these facts.

But for the benefit of those who have yet to acquire a knowledge of this extraordinary people, I advise, first, a visit to the Museum at Teheran in order to excite their interest in the subject, and second, the reading of such books as Nofuhl's "What we Found in the West," and Noz-yt-ahl's "History of the Mehrikans." The last-named is a complete and reliable history of these people from the birth of the Republic under George-wash-yn-tun to the year 1990, when they ceased to exist as a nation. I must say, however, that Noz-yt-ahl leaves the reader much confused concerning the period between the massacre of the Protestants in 1927, and the overflow of the Murfey dynasty in 1940.

He holds the opinion with many other historians that the Mehrikans were a mongrel race, with little or no patriotism, and were purely imitative; simply an enlarged copy of other nationalities extant at the time. He pronounces them a shallow, nervous,

---

13 **antiquity** [æn'tɪkwət̬i] ancient past – 26 **mongrel** of mixed descent – 28 **extant** existing, present

extravagant people, and accords them but few redeeming virtues. This, of course, is just; but nevertheless they will always be an interesting study by reason of their rapid growth, their vast numbers, their marvellous mechanical ingenuity and their sudden and almost unaccountable disappearance.

The wealth, luxury, and gradual decline of the native population; the frightful climatic changes which swept the country like a mower's scythe; the rapid conversion of a vast continent, alive with millions of pleasure-loving people, into a silent wilderness, where the sun and moon look down in turn upon hundreds of weed-grown cities; all this is told by Noz-yt-ahl with force and accuracy.

"Here's Truth. 'Tis a bitter pill but good physic."

8 **scythe** [saɪð] *Sense* – 11 **Noz-yt-ahl** "Knows it all"

ABOARD THE ZLOTUHB IN THE YEAR 2951

10th May

There is land ahead!

Grip-til-lah was first to see it, and when he shouted the tidings my heart beat fast with joy. The famished crew have forgotten their disconsolate stomachs and are dancing about the deck. 'Tis not I, forsooth, who shall restrain them! A month of emptiness upon a heavy sea is preparation for any folly. Nofuhl alone is without enthusiasm. The old man's heart seems dead.

We can see the land plainly, a dim strip along the western horizon. A fair wind blows from the northeast, but we get on with cruel hindrance, for the Zlotuhb is a heavy ship, her bluff bow and voluminous bottom ill fitting her for speed.

11th May

Sighted a fine harbor this afternoon, and are now at anchor in it. Grip-til-lah thinks we have reached an island mentioned by Ben-a-Bout. Nofuhl, however, is sure we are further North.

12th May

What a change has come over Nofuhl! He is the youngest man aboard. We all share his delight, as our discoveries are truly marvellous. This morning while I was yet in my bunk he ran into the cabin and, forgetting our difference in rank, seized me by the arm and tried to drag me out. His excitement so had the better of him that I captured little meaning from his words. Hastening after him, however, I was amazed to see such ancient limbs transport a man so rapidly. He skipped up the narrow stairs like a heifer and, young though I am, it was faster than I could follow.

---

5 **famished** starving, hungry – 6 **disconsolate** unhappy, miserable – 7 **forsooth** *(old)* honestly – 26 **heifer** ['hefɚ] young cow

But what a sight when I reached the deck! We saw nothing of it yesterday, for the dusk of evening was already closing about us when we anchored.

Right ahead, in the middle of the bay, towered a gigantic statue, many times higher than the masts of our ship. Beyond, from behind this statue, came the broad river upon whose waters we were floating, its surface all a-glitter with the rising sun. To the East, where Nofuhl was pointing, his fingers trembling with excitement, lay the ruins of an endless city. It stretched far away into the land beyond, further even than our eyes could see. And in the smaller river on the right stood two colossal structures, rising high in the air, and standing like twin brothers, as if to guard the deserted streets beneath. Not a sound reached us; not a floating thing disturbed the surface of the water. Verily, it seemed the sleep of Death.

I was lost in wonder.

As we looked, a strange bird, like a heron, arose with a hoarse cry from the foot of the great image and flew toward the city.

"What does it all mean?" I cried. "Where are we?"

"Where indeed!" said Nofuhl. "If I knew but that, O Prince, I could tell the rest! No traveller has mentioned these ruins. Persian history contains no record of such a people. Allah has decreed that we discover a forgotten world."

Within an hour we landed, and found ourselves in an ancient street, the pavements covered with weeds, grass, and flowers, all crowding together in wild neglect. Huge trees of great antiquity thrust their limbs through windows and roofs and produced a mournful sight. They gave a welcome shade, however, as we find the heat ashore of a roasting quality most hard to bear. The curious buildings on either

11 **colossal** incredibly huge or giant – 14 **verily** *(old)* truly

side are wonderfully preserved, even sheets of glass still standing in many of the iron window-frames.

We wandered along through the thick grass, Nofuhl and I, much excited over our discoveries and delighted with the strange scene. The sunshine is of dazzling brightness, birds are singing everywhere, and the ruins are gay with gorgeous wild flowers. We soon found ourselves in what was once a public square, now for the most part a shady grove.

THE CITY OF RUINS

(Afterward ascertained to be the square of the City Hall.)

As we sat on a fallen cornice and gazed on the lofty buildings about us I asked Nofuhl if he was still in ignorance as to where we were, and he said:

---

9 **ascertained** determined, discovered – 10 **cornice** *Gesims*

"As yet I know not. The architecture is much like that of ancient Europe, but it tells us nothing."

Then I said to him in jest, "Let this teach us, O Nofuhl! the folly of excessive wisdom. Who among thy pupils of the Imperial College at Ispahan would believe their venerable instructor in history and languages could visit the largest city in the world and know so little about it!"

"Thy words are wise, my Prince," he answered; "few babes could know less."

As we were leaving this grove my eyes fell upon an upturned slab that seemed to have a meaning. It was lying at our feet, partly hidden by the tall grass, having fallen from the columns that supported it. Upon its surface were strange characters in bold relief, as sharp and clear as when chiselled ten centuries ago. I pointed it out to Nofuhl, and we bent over it with eager eyes.

It was this:

ASTOR HOUSE

"The inscription is Old English," he said. "'House' signified a dwelling, but the word 'Astor' I know not. It was probably the name of a deity, and here was his temple."

This was encouraging, and we looked about eagerly for other signs.

Our steps soon brought us into another street, and as we walked I expressed my surprise at the wonderful preservation of the stone work, which looked as though cut but yesterday.

"In such an atmosphere decay is slow," said Nofuhl. "A thousand years at least have passed since these houses were occupied. Take yonder oak, for instance; the tree itself has been growing for at least

---

5 **venerable** honored, esteemed, highly respected – 17 **Astor House** probably a reference to the first luxury hotel in New York City – 20 **deity** ['di:əti] god, goddess

a hundred years, and we know from the fallen mass beneath it that centuries had gone by before its birth was possible."

He stopped speaking, his eyes fixed upon an inscription over a doorway, partly hidden by one of the branches of the oak.

Turning suddenly upon me with a look of triumph, he exclaimed:

"It is ours!"

"What is ours?" I asked.

"The knowledge we sought;" and he pointed to the inscription,

NEW YORK STOCK EXC...

He was tremulous with joy.

"Thou hast heard of Nhu-Yok, O my Prince?"

I answered that I had read of it at school.

"Thou art in it now!" he said. "We are standing on the Western Continent. Little wonder we thought our voyage long!"

"And what was Nhu-Yok?" I asked. "I read of it at college, but remember little. Was it not the capital of the ancient Mehrikans?"

"Not the capital," he answered, "but their largest city. Its population was four millions."

"Four millions!" I exclaimed. "Verily, O Fountain of Wisdom, that is many for one city!"

"Such is history, my Prince! Moreover, as thou knowest, it would take us many days to walk this town."

"True, it is endless."

He continued thus:

"Strange that a single word can tell so much! Those iron structures, the huge statue in the harbor, the temples with pointed towers, all are as writ in history."

---

3 inscription engraving, carving – **11 tremulous** shaking excitedly

Whereupon I repeated that I knew little of the Mehrikans save what I had learned at college, a perfunctory and fleeting knowledge, as they were a people who interested me but little.

"Let us seat ourselves in the shade," said Nofuhl, "and I will tell thee of them."

We sat.

"For eleven centuries the cities of this sleeping hemisphere have decayed in solitude. Their very existence has been forgotten. The people who built them have long since passed away, and their civilization is but a shadowy tradition. Historians are astounded that a nation of an hundred million beings should vanish from the earth like a mist, and leave so little behind. But to those familiar with their lives and character, surprise is impossible. There was nothing to leave. The Mehrikans possessed neither literature, art, nor music

IN A STREET OF THE FORGOTTEN CITY

2 perfunctory uninterested, brief

of their own. Everything was borrowed. The very clothes they wore were copied with ludicrous precision from the models of other nations. They were a sharp, restless, quick-witted, greedy race, given body and soul to the gathering of riches. Their chiefest passion was to buy and sell. Even women, both of high and low degree, spent much of their time at bargains, crowding and jostling each other in vast marts of trade, for their attire was complicated, and demanded most of their time."

"How degrading!" I exclaimed.

"So it must have been," said Nofuhl; "but they were not without virtues. Their domestic life was happy. A man had but one wife, and treated her as his equal."

"That is curious! But as I remember, they were a people of elastic honor."

"They were so considered," said Nofuhl; "their commercial honor was a jest. They were sharper than the Turks. Prosperity was their god, with cunning and invention for his prophets. Their restless activity no Persian can comprehend. This vast country was alive with noisy industries, the nervous Mehrikans darting with inconceivable rapidity from one city to another by a system of locomotion we can only guess at. There existed roads with iron rods upon them, over which small houses on wheels were drawn with such velocity that a long day's journey was accomplished in an hour. Enormous ships without sails, driven by a mysterious force, bore hundreds of people at a time to the farthermost points of the earth."

"And are these things lost?" I asked.

"We know many of the forces," said Nofuhl, "but the knowledge, of applying them is gone. The very elements seem to have been their slaves. Cities were illuminated at night by artificial moons, whose

2 ludicrous ridiculous, foolish – **13 elastic** flexible, adaptable radiance eclipsed the moon above. Strange devices were in use by which they conversed together when separated by a journey of many days. Some of these appliances exist to-day in Persian museums. The superstitions of our ancestors allowed their secrets to be lost during those dark centuries from which at last we are waking."

At this point we heard the voice of Bhoz-ja-khaz in the distance; they had found a spring and he was calling to us.

Such heat we had never felt, and it grew hotter each hour. Near the river where we ate it was more comfortable, but even there the perspiration stood upon us in great drops. Our faces shone like fishes. It was our wish to explore further, but the streets were like ovens, and we returned to the Zlotuhb.

As I sat upon the deck this afternoon recording the events of the morning in this journal Bhoz-ja-khaz and Ad-el-pate approached, asking permission to take the small boat and visit the great statue. Thereupon Nofuhl informed us that this statue in ancient times held aloft a torch illuminating the whole harbor, and he requested Ad-el-pate to try and discover how the light was accomplished.

They returned toward evening with this information: that the statue is not of solid bronze, but hollow; that they ascended by means of an iron stairway into the head of the image, and from the top looked down upon us; that Ad-el-pate, in the dark, sat to rest himself upon a nest of yellow flies with black stripes; that these flies inserted stings into Ad-el-pate's person, causing him to exclaim loudly and descend the stairs with unexpected agility; that Bhoz-ja-khaz and the others pushed on through the upraised arm, and stood at last upon the bronze torch itself; that the city lay beneath them like a map, covering the country for miles away on both sides of the river. As for illuminating the harbor, Bhoz-ja-khaz says Nofuhl is

1 **eclipsed** blocked out – 25 **agility** ability to move quickly and easily

mistaken; there are no vestiges of anything that could give a light; no vessel for oil or traces of fire.

Nofuhl says Ja-khaz is an idiot; that he shall go himself.

13th May

A startling discovery this morning.

By landing higher up the river we explored a part of the city where the buildings are of a different character from those we saw yesterday. Nofuhl considers them the dwellings of the rich. In shape they are like bricks set on end, all very similar, uninteresting, and monotonous.

We noticed one where the doors and shutters were still in place, but rotting from the fantastic hinges that supported them. A few hard blows brought down the outer doors in a dusty heap, and as we stepped upon the marble floor within our eyes met an unexpected sight.

Furniture, statues, dingy pictures in crumbling frames, images in bronze and silver, mirrors, curtains, all were there, but in every condition of decay. We knocked open the iron shutters and let the light into the rooms sealed up for centuries. In the first one lay a rug from Persia! Faded, moth-eaten, gone in places, it seemed to ask us with dying eyes to be taken hence. My heart grew soft over the ancient rug, and I caught a foolish look in Lev-el-Hedyd's eye.

As we climbed the mouldering stair to the floor above I expressed surprise that cloth and woodwork should hold together for so many centuries, also saying:

"These Mehrikans were not so unworthy as we think them."

"That may be," said Lev-el-Hedyd, "but the Persian rug is far the freshest object we have seen, and that perchance was ancient when they bought it."

---

1 **vestige** ['vestɪʤ] remnant, sign, trace – 10 **monotonous** [mə'nɑːt̬ᵊnəs] boring, lacking in variety

On this floor we entered a dim chamber, spacious and once richly furnished. When Lev-el-Hedyd pushed open the shutters and drew aside the ragged curtains we started at the sight before us.

Upon a wide bed in the centre of the room lay a human form, the long, yellow hair still clinging to the head. It was more a mummy than a skeleton. Around, upon the bed, lay mouldering fragments of the once white sheets that covered it. On the fingers of the left hand glistened two rings which drew our attention. One held a

IN THE MOULDERING CHAMBER

6 **mouldering** decaying, rotting

diamond of great price, the other was composed of sapphires and diamonds most curiously arranged. We stood a moment in silence, gazing sadly upon the figure.

"Poor woman," I said, "left thus to die alone."

"It is more probable," said Nofuhl, "she was already dead, and her friends, departing perhaps in haste, were unable to burn the body."

"Did they burn their dead?" I asked. "In my history 'twas writ they buried them in the earth like potatoes, and left them to rot."

And Nofuhl answered: "At one time it was so, but later on, as they became more civilized, the custom was abandoned."

"Is it possible?" I asked, "that this woman has been lying here almost a thousand years and yet so well preserved?"

"I, also, am surprised," said Nofuhl. "I can only account for it by the extreme dryness of the air in absorbing the juices of the body and retarding decay."

Then lifting tenderly in his hand some of the yellow hair, he said: "She was probably very young, scarce twenty."

"Were their women fair?" I asked.

"They were beautiful," he answered; "with graceful forms and lovely faces; a pleasure to the eye; also were they gay and sprightly with much animation."

Thereupon cried Lev-el-Hedyd:

"Here are the first words thou hast uttered, O Nofuhl, that cause me to regret the extinction of this people! There is ever a place in my heart for a blushing maiden!"

"Then let thy grief be of short life," responded Nofuhl, "for Mehrikan damsels were not of that description. Blushing was an art they practised little. The shyness thou so lovest in a Persian maiden was to them an unknown thing. Our shrinking daughters

---

16 **retarding** slowing down – 21 **sprightly** full of energy, active

bear no resemblance to these Western products. They strode the public streets with roving eyes and unblushing faces, holding free converse with men as with women, bold of speech and free of manner, going and coming as it pleased them best. They knew much of the world, managed their own affairs, and devised their own marriages, often changing their minds and marrying another than the betrothed."

"Bismillah! And men could love these things?" exclaimed Lev-el-Hedyd with much feeling.

"So it appears."

"But I should say the Mehrikan bride had much the freshness of a dried fig."

"So she had," said Nofuhl; "but those who know only the dried fig have no regret for the fresh fruit. But the fault was not with the maidens. Brought up like boys, with the same studies and mental development, the womanly part of their nature gradually vanished as their minds expanded. Vigor of intellect was the object of a woman's education."

Then Lev-el-Hedyd exclaimed with great disgust:

"Praises be to Allah for his aid in exterminating such a people!" and he walked away from the bed, and began looking about the chamber. In a moment he hastened back to us, saying:

"Here are more jewels! Also money!"

Nofuhl eagerly took the pieces.

"Money!" he cried. "Money will tell us more than pages of history!"

There were silver coins of different sizes and two small pieces of copper. Nofuhl studied them closely.

---

7 **betrothed** *(old)* person to whom one is engaged to be married – 17 **vigor** here: strength, hardiness – 20 **to exterminate** to kill or destroy; *usu* refers to insects or rodents

THE FACE AND BACK OF ONE OF THE SILVER COINS

"The latest date is 1957," he said; "a little less than a thousand years ago; but the piece may have been in circulation some years before this woman died; also it may have been coined the very year of her death. It bears the head of Dennis, the last of the Hy-Burnyan dictators. The race is supposed to have become extinct before 1990 of their era."

I then said;

"Thou hast never told us, O Nofuhl, the cause of their disappearance!"

"There were many causes," he answered. "The Mehrikans themselves were of English origin, but people from all parts of Europe came here in vast numbers. Although the original comers were vigorous and hardy; the effect of climate upon succeeding generations was fatal. They became flat-chested and thin, with scanty hair, fragile teeth, and weak digestions. Nervous diseases unknown to us wrought deadly havoc.

---

16 **wrought** [rɑːt] inflicted, caused

Children were reared with difficulty. Between 1945 and 1960, the last census of which any record remains, the population decreased from ninety millions to less than twelve millions. Climatic changes, the like of which no other land ever experienced, began at that period, and finished in less than ten years a work made easy by nervous natures and rapid lives. The temperature would skip in a single day from burning heat to winter's cold. No constitution could withstand it, and this vast continent became once more an empty wilderness."

Much more of the same nature he told us, but I am too sleepy to write longer. We explored the rest of the mansion, finding many things of interest. I caused several objects to be carried aboard the Zlotuhb.

(These objects are now in the museum of the Imperial College, at Teheran.)

14th May

Hotter than yesterday.

In the afternoon we were rowed up the river and landed for a short walk. It is unsafe to brave the sun.

The more I learn of these Mehrikans the less interesting they become. Nofuhl is of much the same mind, judging from our conversation to-day, as we walked along together. It was in this wise:

Khan-li: How alike the houses! How monotonous!

Nofuhl: So, also, were the occupants. They thought alike, worked alike, ate, dressed and conversed alike. They read the same books; they fashioned their garments as directed, with no regard for the size or figure of the individual, and copied to a stitch the fashions of Europeans.

---

7 **constitution** here: body, structure – 26 **to converse** to talk with each other

Khan-li: But the close-fitting apparel of the European must have been sadly uncomfortable in the heat of a Mehrikan summer.

Nofuhl: So probably it was. Stiff boxes of varying patterns adorned the heads of men. Curious jackets with tight sleeves compressed the body. The feet throbbed and burned in close-fitting casings of un-yielding leather, and linen made stiff by artificial means was drawn tightly about the neck.

Khan-li: Allah! What idiots!

Nofuhl: Even so are they considered.

Khan-li: To what quality of their minds do you attribute such love of needless suffering?

Nofuhl: It was their desire to be like others. A natural feeling in a vulgar people.

15th May

A fair wind from the West to-day. We weighed anchor and sailed up the Eastern side of the city. I did this as Nofuhl finds the upper portion of the town much richer in relics than the lower, which seems to have been given up to commercial purposes. We sailed close under one of the great monuments in the river, and are at a loss to divine its meaning. Many iron rods still dangle from the tops of each of the structures. As they are in a line, one with the other, we thought at first they might have been once connected and served as a bridge, but we soon saw they were too far apart.

---

6 **un-yielding** solid, inflexible – 9 **even so** exactly this way – 15 **weigh anchor** pull up the anchor of a ship and move off, start your journey on a ship

THE TWO MONUMENTS IN THE RIVER

Came to anchor about three miles from the old mooring. Up the river and down, North, South, East, and West, the ruins stretch away indefinitely, seemingly without end. Am anxious about Lev-el-Hedyd. He went ashore and has not returned. It is now after midnight.

16th May

Praise Allah! my dear comrade is alive! This morning we landed early and began our search for him. As we passed before the building which bears the inscription DORF ASTORIA upon its front, we heard his voice from within in answer to our calls.

We entered, and after climbing the ruined stairway found him seated upon the floor above. He had a swollen leg from an ugly sprain, and various bruises were also his. While our friends were constructing a litter on which to bear him hence we conversed together. The walls about us bore traces of having once enclosed a hall of some beauty. In idling about I pulled open the decaying door of an old closet and saw upon the rotting shelves many pieces of glass and earthenware of fine workmanship. Taking one in my hand, a small wine-cup of glass, I approached my comrade calling his attention to its slender stem and curious form. As his eyes fell upon it they opened wide in amazement.

FINE WORKMANSHIP

I also observed a trembling of his hand as he reached forth to touch it. He then recounted to me his marvellous adventure of the night before, but saying before he began:

"Thou knowest, O Prince, I am no believer in visions, and I should never tell the tale but for thy discovery of this cup. I drank from such an one last night, proffered by a ghostly hand."

9 litter stretcher used to carry injured people

I would have smiled, but he was much in earnest. As I made a movement to sit beside him, he said: “Taste first, O my master, of the grapes hanging from yonder wall.”

I did so, and to my great surprise found them of an exquisite flavor, finer even than the cultivated fruit of Persia, sweeter and more delicate, of a different nature from the wild grapes we have been eating. My astonishment appeared to delight him, and he said with a laugh: “The grapes are impossible, but they exist; even more absurd is my story!” and he then narrated his adventure.

It was this:

WHAT LEV-EL-HEDYD SAW.

Yesterday, after nightfall, as he was hastening toward the Zlotuhb he fell violently upon some blocks of stone, wrenching his ankle and much bruising himself. Unable to walk upon his foot he limped into this building to await our coming in the morning. The howling of wolves and other wild beasts as they prowled about the city drove him, for safety, to crawl up the ruins of the stairway to the floor above. As he settled himself in a corner of this hall his nostrils were greeted with the delicious odor from the grapes about his head. He found them surprisingly good, and ate heartily. He soon after fell into a sleep which lasted some hours, for when he awoke the moon was higher in the heavens, the voices of the wolves were hushed and the city was silent.

As he lay in a revery, much absorbed in his own thoughts, he gradually became aware of mysterious changes taking place, as if by stealth, about him. A decorated ceiling appeared to be closing over the hall. Mirrors and tinted walls slowly crept in place of ivy and crumbling bricks. A faint glow grew stronger and more intense until it filled the great room with a dazzling light.

---

1 **earnest** [ˈɜːrnɪst] serious, intense – 13 **wrenching** twisting, spraining – 26 **stealth** [steθ] covertness, sneakiness

Then came softly into view a table of curious form, set out with flowers and innumerable dishes of glass and porcelain, as for a feast.

Standing about the room he saw solemn men with beardless faces, all in black attire, whose garments bore triangular openings upon the chest to show the shirt beneath. These personages he soon discovered were servants.

As he gazed in bewilderment, there entered other figures, two by two, who took their seats about the table. These later comers, sixty or more, were men and women walking arm in arm, the women in rich attire of unfamiliar fashion and sparkling with precious stones. The men were clad like the servants.

They ate and drank and laughed, and formed a brilliant scene. Lev-el-Hedyd rose to his feet, and moved by a curiosity he made no effort to resist, for he is a reckless fellow and knows no fear – he hobbled out into the room.

They looked upon him in surprise, and seemed much amused at his presence. One of the guests, a tall youth with yellow mustaches, approached him, offering a delicate crystal vessel filled with a sparkling fluid.

Lev-el-Hedyd took it.

The youth raised another from the table and with a slight gesture as if in salutation, he said in words which my comrade understood, though he swears it was a language unknown to him,

“We may meet again the fourth of next month.”

He then drank the wine, and so did Lev-el-Hedyd.

Hereupon the others smiled as if at their comrade’s wit, all save the women, whose tender faces spoke more of pity than of mirth. The wine flew to his brain as he drank it, and things about him seemed to reel and spin. Strains of fantastic music burst upon his

---

8 **bewilderment** shocked surprise – 23 **salutation** greeting, welcome

ears: then, all in rhythm, the women joined their partners and whirled about him with a lightsome step. And, moving with it, his throbbing brain seemed dancing from his head. The room itself, all swaying and quivering with the melody, grew dim and stole from view. The music softly died away.

Again was silence, the moon above looking calmly down upon the ivied walls.

He fell like a drunken man upon the floor, and did not wake till our voices called him.

Such his tale.

He has a clear head and is no liar, but so many grapes upon an empty stomach with the fever from his swollen limb might well explain it.

■

Bear's meat for dinner.

This morning toward noon Kuzundam, the second officer, wandered on ahead of us, and entered a large building in pursuit of a rabbit. He was about descending to the basement below, when he saw, close before him, a bear leisurely mounting the marble stairs. Kuzundam is no coward, but he turned and ran as he never ran before. The bear, who seemed of a sportive nature, also ran, and in close pursuit. Luckily for my friend we happened to be near, otherwise instead of our eating bear's meat, the bear might have lunched quietly off Kuzundam in the shady corridors of the "FIFTH AVENUE HOTEL."

KUZUNDAM'S NARROW ESCAPE

17th May

Today a scorching heat that burns the lungs. We started in the morning prepared to spend the night ashore, and explore the northern end of the city. It was a pleasant walk through the soft grass of the shady streets, but in those places unsheltered from the sun we were as fish upon a frying-pan. Other dwellings we saw, even larger and more imposing than the one we entered yesterday. We were tempted to explore them, but Lev-el-Hedyd wisely dissuaded us, saying the day was waxing hotter each hour and it could be done on our return.

In the northern part of the town are many religious temples, with their tall towers like slender pyramids, tapering to a point. They are curious things, and surprisingly well preserved. The interiors of these temples are uninteresting. Nofuhl says the religious rites of

8 **dissuade** convince not to do sth

the Mehrikans were devoid of character. There were many religious beliefs, all complicated and insignificant variations one from another, each sect having its own temples and refusing to believe as the others. This is amusing to a Persian, but mayhap was a serious matter with them. One day in each week they assembled, the priests reading long moral lectures written by themselves, with music by hired singers. They then separated, taking no thought of temple or priest for another seven days. Nofuhl says they were not a religious people. That the temples were filled mostly with women.

IN ONE OF THE TEMPLES

In the afternoon we found it necessary to traverse a vast pleasure-ground, now a wild forest, but with traces still visible of broad promenades and winding drive-ways. (Olbaldeh thinks this must be the Centralpahk sometimes alluded to in Mehrikan literature.) There remains an avenue of bronze statues, most of them yet upright and in good condition, but very comic. Lev-el-Hedyd and I still think them caricatures, but Nofuhl is positive they were

2 **devoid of** *(old)* without – 13 **mayhap** maybe, possibly

serious efforts, and says the Mehrikans were easily pleased in matters of art.

We lost our way in this park, having nothing to guide us as in the streets of the city. This was most happy, as otherwise we should have missed a surprising discovery.

It occurred in this wise.

Being somewhat overcome by the heat we halted upon a little hill to rest ourselves. While reclining beneath the trees I noticed unusual carvings upon a huge block against which Lev-el-Hedyd was supporting his back. They were unlike any we had seen, and yet they were not unfamiliar. As I lay there gazing idly at them it flashed upon me they were Egyptian. We at once fell to examining the block, and found to our amazement an obelisk of Egyptian granite, covered with Egyptian hieroglyphics of an antiquity exceeding by thousands of years the most ancient monuments of the country!

Verily, we were puzzled!

"When did the Egyptians invade Mehrika?" quoth Bhoz-ja-khaz, with a solemn look, as if trying to recall a date.

"No Egyptian ever heard of Mehrika," said Nofuhl. "This obelisk was finished twenty centuries before the first Mehrikan was weaned. In all probability it was brought here as a curiosity, just as we take to Persia the bronze head of George-wash-yn-tun."

We spent much time over the monument, and I think Nofuhl was disappointed that he could not bring it away with him.

Also while in this park we came to a high tower, standing by itself, and climbed to the top, where we enjoyed a wide-spreading view.

The extent of the city is astounding.

Miles away in the river lay the Zlotuhb, a white speck on the water. All about us in every direction as far as sight can reach were

---

6 **in this wise** *(old)* in this way; like this – 13 **obelisk** ['ɑ:bᵊlɪsk]

ruins, and ruins, and ruins. Never was a more melancholy sight. The blue sky, the bright sunshine, the sweet-scented air with the gay flowers and singing birds only made it sadder. They seemed a mockery.

We have encamped for the night, and I can write no more. Countless flying insects gather about us with a hateful buzz, and bite us beyond endurance. They are a pest thrice accursed.

I tell Nofuhl his fine theory concerning the extinction of the Yahnkis is a good tale for those who have never been here.

No man without a leather skin could survive a second night.

18th May

Poor Ja-khaz is worse than sick.

He had an encounter last night with a strange animal, and his defeat was ignoble. The animal, a pretty thing, much like a kitten, was hovering near when Ja-khaz, with rare courage and agility, threw himself upon it.

And then what happened none of us can state with precision. We know we held our noses and fled. And Ja-khaz! No words can fit him. He carries with him an odor to devastate a province. We had to leave him ashore and send him fresh raiment.

This is, verily, a land of surprises.

Our hands and faces still smart from the biting insects, and the perfume of the odorous kitten promises to be ever with us.

Nofuhl is happy. We have discovered hundreds of metal blocks, the poorest of which he asserts would be the gem of a museum. They were found by Fattan-laiz-eh in the basement of a high building, all laid carefully away upon iron shelves. The flood of light they throw

1 **melancholy** sad, gloomy – 7 **thrice accursed** cursed three times, roots in Middle English – 14 **ignoble** shameful, dishonorable – 20 **raiment** clothing

upon the manners and customs of this ludicrous people renders them of priceless value to historians.

I harbor a suspicion that it causes Nofuhl some pleasure to sit upon the cool deck of the Ziotuhb and watch Bhoz-ja-khaz walking to and fro upon the ruins of a distant wharf.

19th May

The air is cooler. Grip-til-lah thinks a storm is brewing.

Even Nofuhl is puzzled over the wooden image we brought aboard yesterday. It is well preserved, with the barbaric coloring still fresh upon it. They found it standing upright in a little shop.

How these idols were worshipped, and why they are found in little shops and never in the great temples is a mystery. It has a diadem of feathers on the head, and as we sat smoking upon the deck this evening I remarked to Nofuhl that it might be the portrait of some Mehrikan noble. Whereupon he said they had no nobles.

THE WOODEN GOD

"But the Mehrikans of gentle blood," I asked, "had they no titles?"

27 **gentle** here: noble, distinguished

"Neither titles nor gentle blood," he answered. "And as they were all of much the same origin, and came to this country simply to thrive more fatly than at home, there was nothing except difference in wealth on which to establish a superior order. Being deep respecters of money this was a satisfying distinction. It soon resulted that those families who possessed riches for a generation or two became the substitute for an aristocracy. This upper class was given to sports and pastimes, spending their wealth freely, being prodigiously fond of display. Their intellectual development was feeble, and they wielded but little influence save in social matters. They followed closely the fashions of foreign aristocracies. Great attentions were paid to wandering nobles from other lands. Even distant relatives of titled people were greeted with the warmest enthusiasm."

Then I said to him, "But explain to me, O Nofuhl, how it was possible for so shallow a nation to become so great."

"They were great only in numbers and too weak to endure success. At the beginning of the twentieth century – as they counted time – huge fortunes were amassed in a day, and the Mehrikans became drunk with money."

Whereupon I exclaimed, "O Land of Delight! For much money is cheering."

But the old man shook his head. "Very true, O Prince; but the effect was woful. These vast fortunes soon dominated all things, even the seat of government and the courts of Justice. Tricks of finance brought fabulous gains. Young men became demoralized. For sober industry with its moderate profits was ridiculed."

"Verily, that would be natural!" I said. "But in a land where all were rich who was found to cook and scrub, to fetch and carry and

---

7 **aristocracy** [ˌərəˈstɑːkrəsi] *Adelsherrschaft* – 9 **prodigiously** [prəˈdɪʤəsli] abnormally, greatly – 24 **woful** sad, mournful, terrible

to till the soil? For none will shovel earth when his pockets are stuffed with gold."

"All were not rich. And when the poor also became greedy they became hostile. Then began social upheavals with bloodshed and havoc."

20th May

An icy wind from the northeast with a violent rain. Yesterday we gasped with the hot air. To-day we are shivering in winter clothing.

21st May

The same as yesterday. Most of us are ill. My teeth chatter and my body is both hot and cold. A storm more wicked never wailed about a ship. Lev-el-Hedyd calls it the shrieking voices of the hundred millions of Mehrikans who must have perished in similar weather.

16th June

It is many days since I have touched this journal. A hateful sickness has been upon me, destroying all energy and courage. A sort of fever, and yet my limbs were cold. I could not describe it if I would.

Nofuhl came into the cabin this evening with some of his metal plates and discoursed upon them. He has no respect for the intellects of the early Mehrikans. I thought for a moment I had caught him in a contradiction, but he was right as usual. It was thus:

Nofuhl: They were great readers.

Khan-li: You have told us they had no literature. Were they great readers of nothing?

Nofuhl: Verily, thou hast said it! Vast sheets of paper were published daily in which all crimes were recorded in detail. The more revolting the deed, the more minute the description. Horrors

---

28 minute (*adj*) [maɪˈnuːt] *here:* detailed, precise

were their chief delight. Scandals were drunk in with thirstful eyes. These chronicles of crime and filth were issued by hundreds of thousands. There was hardly a family in the land but had one.

Khan-li: And did this take the place of literature.

Nofuhl: Even so.

20th June

Once more we are on the sea; two days from Nhu-Yok. Our decision was a sudden one. Nofuhl, in an evil moment, found among those accursed plates a map of the country, and thereupon was seized with an unreasoning desire to visit a town called "Washington." I wavered and at last consented, foolishly I believe, for the crew are loud for Persia. And this town is inland on a river. He says it was their finest city, the seat of Government, the capital of the country. Grip-til-lah swears he can find it if the map is truthful.

Ja-khaz still eats by himself.

This afternoon we reclined upon the deck, the Zlotuhb drifting gently in a southerly direction. Land could be seen on the starboard bow, a faint strip along the western horizon.

It was about the middle of the afternoon, while passing the ruins of a gigantic tower – perhaps a lighthouse – that Nofuhl, of a sudden, clambered hastily to his feet and looked about him. Then he called to Grip-til-lah, asking how many leagues we were from the harbor of Nhu-Yok. Grip-til-lah's reply I forget, but it filled the old man with a gentle excitement. I observed an unwonted sparkle in his eyes, also a quivering of the fingers as he pointed to the ocean around about, and exclaimed:

---

5 **Even so** *(old)* Yes, that's right/true. – 22 **league** [li:g] *(old)* unit of length, distance a person could walk in one hour – 24 **unwonted** unusual, strange

"Beneath us, the bottom of the sea is covered with iron ships – the wrecks of stupendous navies – the mightiest of all human history!"

At once we all became interested.

"What navies?" I inquired. "And what compassed their destruction? Was it a battle?"

Nofuhl: A battle of whose magnitude no Persian has conception; a conflict in which the sea was tossed and the heavens rent by thunderings of iron monsters. Any one of them would have blown to atoms a fleet of Zlotuhbs.

Ad-el-pate: Verily! A tale easier told than believed. But I would readily venture my head in the Zlotuhb against any of these nursery-tale wonders.

Nofuhl: And with wisdom. For the loss of thy brain. Ad-el-pate, could not affect the nature of thy speech.

Whereupon there was laughter, and Ad-el-pate held his peace.

Khan-li: But tell us of this battle, O Nofuhl. I remember now to have read about it at college. These details of ancient history I am prone to forget. How came it about?

Nofuhl: I have spoken of the Mehrikans being a greedy race. And their greed, at last, resulted in this war. By means of one-sided laws of their own making they secured for themselves a lion's share of all profits from the world's commerce. This checked the prosperity of other nations, until at last the leading powers of Europe combined in self-defence against this all-absorbing greed. They collected an armada the like of which was never imagined, neither before nor since. Then, across the ocean, came the iron host. And here, upon this very spot where we are floating, they met the Mehrikan ships.

Khan-li: How many ships in all?

---

5 **compassed** here: brought about, achieved – 26 **armada** fleet or squad of warships

Nofuhl: The Mehrikans had eighty heavy ships of iron, with a number of smaller craft. The allies had two hundred and forty heavy battleships, all of iron. They also had smaller craft for diverse purposes.

Khan-li: Allah! A bad prospect for our greedy friends! And being a nation of traders they had no liking, probably, for the perils of war.

Nofuhl: As to that historians differ. According to the Mehrikans themselves they were mighty warriors. But certain writers of that period give a different impression. Noz-yt-ahl is sure they were cowards, weak in body as in spirit, but often favored by fortune. In my opinion, this battle throws considerable light upon that matter.

A day like this, it was, also in June, as the Europeans, coming northward along the coast to seize Nhu-Yok, met the Mehrikan Admiral Nev-r-sai-di with his eighty ships. And the struggle was short.

Khan-li: Verily, I can believe it! With three ships to one I would give the Europeans about half a day – a summer afternoon like this – to send the greedy ones to the bottom.

Nofuhl: Thy guess is good, O Prince, as to the hours of fighting. It lasted just one summer afternoon. But the Mehrikans it was who sent their enemies to the bottom. And the sea beneath our feet is strewn with iron hulks.

Khan-li: Bismillah! If that be a true tale – and I doubt it not – these greedy ones were not so contemptible, at least when there was profit in it.

Lev-el-Hedyd: At what period did this occur?

Nofuhl: Early in the twentieth century. I cannot recall the date, but it was never forgotten by the Mehrikans. Surely a just pride, for

26 **contemptible** horrible, revolting

on that day they accomplished wonders. The Admiral Nev-r-sai-di on his ship the Ztazenztrypes was at one time surrounded by a dozen German men-of-war. And lo! he demolished all! And of Frank and Russyan vessels he put an end to as many more; also sundry Talyans and British.

Lev-el-Hedyd: Bismillah! But that was good! What, O Nofuhl, is the Persian of that name Ztazenztrypes?

Nofuhl: None can tell with certainty. To the Mehrikans it signified victory, or something similar.

Other miracles were achieved by the Mehrikans that day. Noflizon-mee, a little craft with a pointed prow, jammed holes in nearly a score of monster ships, and the waters closed over them. There figured also a long and narrow boat of Mehrikan devising, the Yankyd-Oodl. This astonishing machine sailed to and fro among the foreign ships upsetting all traditions. Much glory befell her commander, the Captain Hoorai-boiz.

Grip-til-lah: And how many ships did the Mehrikans lose?

Nofuhl: Reports are contradictory. According to one of their own writers of the period they suffered no loss whatever in vessels. Yet at the same time he asserts, "We gave them Haleklumbya," which must be the name of a ship.

Khan-li: A gallant fight! But can you explain how such an inferior people could become heroic of a sudden?

Nofuhl: According' to 'Ardfax, an early British historian, they were addicted to surprising feats upon the water. And this statement is borne out by a Spanish admiral, Offulbad-shoota, who maintains that the Mehrikans, being a godless people, were aided by the devil.

---

12 **a score** *(old)* twenty – 25 **feat** trick, skill – 26 **borne out** confirmed

2nd July

We are on the river that leads to "Washington." Grip-til-lah says we shall sight it to-morrow. The river is a dirty color.

3rd July

We see ahead of us the ruins of a great dome, also a very high shaft. Probably they belong to the city we seek.

4th July

A date we shall not forget!

Little did I realize this morning when we left the Zlotuhb in such hilarious mood what dire events awaited us. I landed about noon, accompanied by Nofuhl, Lev-el-Hedyd, Bhoz-ja-khaz, Ad-el-pate, Kuzundam the first mate, Tik'l-palyt the cook, Fattan-laiz-eh, and two sailors. Our march had scarce begun when a startling discovery caused great commotion in our minds. We had halted at Nofuhl's request, to decipher the inscription upon a stone, when Lev-el-Hedyd, who had started on, stopped short with a sudden exclamation. We hastened to him, and there, in the soft earth, was the imprint of human feet!

I cannot describe our surprise. We decided to follow the footprints, and soon found they were leading us toward the great dome more directly than we could have gone ourselves. Our excitement was beyond words. Those of us who had weapons carried them in readiness. The path was little used, but clearly marked. It wound about among fallen fragments and crumbling statues, and took us along a wide avenue between buildings of vast size and solidity, far superior to any we had seen in Nhu-Yok. It seemed a city of monuments.

5 **shaft** tower – 10 **hilarious** happy – 14 **commotion** worry, anxiety – 15 **decipher** decode, translate

THROUGH THE STREETS OF "WASHINGTON"

As we ascended the hill to the great temple and saw it through the trees rising high above us, we were much impressed by its vast size and beauty. Our eyes wandered in admiration over the massive columns, each hewn from a single block, still white and fresh as if newly quarried. The path took us under one of the lower arches of the building, and we emerged upon the other side. This front we found even more beautiful than the one facing the city. At the centre was a flight of steps of magnificent proportions, now falling asunder and overgrown in many places with grass and flowers.

THE RUINS OF THE GREAT TEMPLE

14 **quarried** extracted, obtained *usu* referring to stone – 18 **asunder** apart, to pieces

These steps we ascended. As I climbed silently up, the others following, I saw two human feet, the soles toward us, resting upon the balustrade above. With a gesture I directed Nofuhl's attention to them, and the old man's eyes twinkled with delight. Was it a Mehrikan? I confess to a lively excitement at the prospect of meeting one. How many were they? and how would they treat us?

Looking down upon my little band to see that all were there, I boldly marched up the remaining steps and stood before him.

He was reclining upon a curious little four-legged seat, with his feet upon the balustrade, about on a level with his head. Clad in skins and rough cloth he looked much like a hunter, and he gazed quietly upon me, as though a Persian noble were a daily guest. Such a reception was not gratifying, especially as he remained in the same position, not even withdrawing his feet. He nodded his curious head down once and up again, deeming it apparently a sufficient salutation.

THE FEET UPON THE PORTICO

The maintenance of my own dignity before my followers forbade my standing thus before a seated barbarian, and I made a gesture for him to rise. This he answered in an unseemly manner by ejecting from his mouth a brownish fluid, projecting it over and beyond the

3 **balustrade** railing for balcony or terrace – 22 **gratifying** pleasing, pleasant – 27 **salutation** greeting – 30 **unseemly** impolite

balustrade in front of him. Then looking upon me as if about to laugh, and yet with a grave face, he uttered something in an unmusical voice which I failed to understand.

Upon this, Nofuhl, who had caught the meaning of one or two words, stepped hastily forward and addressed him in his own language. But the barbarian understood with difficulty and they had much trouble in conversing, chiefly from reason of Nofuhl's pronunciation. He afterward told me that this man's language differed but little from that of the Mehrikans, as they wrote it eleven centuries ago.

THE MAN

When he finally arose in talking with Nofuhl I could better observe him. He was tall and bony, with an awkward neck, and appeared at first glance to be a man of forty years. We decided later he was under thirty. His yellow skin and want of hair made him seem much older than he was. I was also much puzzled by the expression of his face. It was one of deep sadness, yet his eyes were full of mirth, and a corner of his mouth was ever drawing up as if in mockery. For myself I liked not his manner. He appeared little impressed by so many strangers, and bore himself as though it were of small importance whether we understood him or not. But Nofuhl since informed me that he asked a multitude of questions concerning us.

What Nofuhl gathered was this:

This Mehrikan with his wife and one old man were all that remained of his race. Thirty-one had died this summer. In ancient

20 **mirth** amusement, cheerfulness – 23 **bore himself** behaved

times there were many millions of his country-men. They were the greatest nation upon the earth. He could not read. He had two names, one was "Jon," the other he had forgotten. They lived in this temple because it was cool. When the temple was built, and for what purpose, he could not tell. He pointed to the West and said the country in that direction was covered with ruined cities.

When Nofuhl told him we were friends, and presented him at my direction with a hunting-knife of fine workmanship, he pushed out his right arm toward me and held it there. For an instant Nofuhl looked at the arm wonderingly, as did we all, then with sudden intelligence he seized the outstretched hand in his own, and moved it up and down. This was interesting, for Nofuhl tells me it was a form of greeting among the ancient Mehrikans.

While all this was going on we had moved into the great circular hall beneath the dome. This hall was of vast proportions, and there were still traces of its former splendor. Against the walls were marble statues entwined in ivy, looking down upon us with melancholy eyes. Here also we met a thin old man, whose hairless head and beardless face almost moved us to mirth.

At Nofuhl's request our host led the way into some of the smaller rooms to show us their manner of living, and it would be impossible to imagine a more pathetic mixture of glory and decay, of wealth and poverty, of civilization and barbarity. Old furniture, dishes of silver, bronze images, even paintings and ornaments of great value were scattered through the rooms, side by side with the most primitive implements. It was plain the ancient arts were long since forgotten.

When we returned to the circular hall our host disappeared for a few moments into a room which he had not shown us. He came back bringing a stone vase with a narrow neck, and was followed by a maiden who bore drinking-cups of copper and tin. These she deposited upon a fallen fragment of the dome which served as a table.

This girl was interesting. A dainty head, delicate features, yellow hair, blue eyes, and a gentle sadness of mien that touched my heart. Had she been ugly, what a different ending to this day!

We all saluted her, and the Mehrikan spoke a few words which we interpreted as a presentation. He filled the cups from the stone vase, and then saying something which Nofuhl failed to catch, he held his cup before his face with a peculiar movement and put it to his lips.

As he did this Lev-el-Hedyd clutched my arm and exclaimed: "The very gesture of the ghost!" And then as if to himself, "And this is July fourth."

But he drank, as did we all, for our thirst was great and the odor of the golden liquid was most alluring. It tasted hotter than the fires of Jelbuz. It was also of great potency and gave a fine exhilaration to the senses. We became happier at once.

And here it was that Ja-khaz did a fatal thing. Being near the maid and much affected by her beauty, he addressed her as Hur-al-missa (The most angelic of women.) which, of course, she understood not. This were well had he gone no further, but he next put his arm about her waist with intent to kiss her. Much terrified, she tried to free herself. But Ja-khaz, holding her fair chin with his other hand, had brought his lips almost to hers when the old man raised his heavy staff and brought it down upon our comrade's head with cruel swiftness. This falling stick upon a solid skull resounded about the dome and echoed through the empty corridors.

Bhoz-ja-khaz blinked and staggered back. Then, with fury in his face, he sprang savagely toward the aged man.

But here the younger Mehrikan interfered. Rapidly approaching them and shutting tight his bony hand, he shot it from him with startling velocity, so directing that it came in contact with the face of Ja-khaz who, to our amazement, sat roughly upon the marble

---

2 mien face, appearance

pavement, the blood streaming from his nostrils. He was a pitiful sight.

Unaccustomed to such warfare we were seriously alarmed, and thought him killed perhaps. Ad-el-pate, a mighty wrestler, and of powerful build, rushed furiously upon the Mehrikan for whom I trembled. But his arm again went out before him, and Ad-el-pate likewise sat. A mournful spectacle, and every Persian felt his heart beat fast within him.

By this time Ja-khaz was on his feet again, purple with rage. With uplifted scimitar he sprang toward our host. The old man stepped between. Ja-khaz, with wanton cruelty, brought his steel upon the ancient head, and stretched him upon the floor. For an instant the younger one stood horror-stricken, then snatching from the floor the patriarch's staff – a heavy stick with an iron end – he jumped forward, and, quicker than words can tell it, dealt a frightful blow

THE SLAUGHTER OF THE PERSIANS

10 **scimitar** ['sɪmɪt̬ɚ] short sword with curved blade *usu* used in Middle Eastern countries

upon the head of Ja-khaz which sent him headlong to the ground with a broken skull.

All this had happened in a moment, and wild confusion followed. My followers drew their arms and rushed upon the Mehrikan. The girl ran forward either from terror or to shield her spouse, I know not which, when a flying arrow from a sailor's cross-bow pierced her to the heart.

This gave the Mehrikan the energy of twenty men.

He knocked brave Kuzundam senseless with a blow that would have killed an ox. Such fury I had not conceived. He brought his flying staff like a thunderbolt from Heaven upon the Persian skulls, yet always edging toward the door to prevent his enemies surrounding him. Four of our number, in as many minutes, joined Ja-khaz upon the floor. Kuzundam, Ad-el-pate, Fattan-laiz-eh, and Ha-tak, a sailor, lay stretched upon the pavement, all dead or grievously wounded.

So suddenly had this taken place, that I hardly realized what had happened. I rushed forward to stay the combat, but he mistook the purpose, struck my scimitar with a force that sent it flying through the air, and had raised his staff to deal a second for myself, when brave Lev-el-Hedyd stepped in to save me, and thrust quickly at him.

But alas! the Mehrikan warded off his stroke with one yet quicker, and brought his stick so swiftly against my comrade's head that it laid him with the others.

When Lev-el-Hedyd fell I saw the Mehrikan had many wounds, for my comrades had made a savage onslaught. He tottered as he moved back into the doorway, where he leaned against the wall for an instant, his eyes meeting ours with a look of defiance and contempt that I would willingly forget. Then the staff dropped from

---

16 **grievously** seriously, gravely – 18 **stay** stop, halt

his hand; he staggered out to the great portico, and fell his length upon the pavement. Nofuhl hastened to him, but he was dead.

As he fell a wonderful thing took place – an impossible thing, as I look back upon it, but both Nofuhl and I saw it distinctly.

THE LAST OF THE MEHRIKANS

In front of the great steps and facing this doorway is a large sitting image of George-wash-yn-tun. As the Mehrikan staggered out upon the porch, his hands outstretched before him and with Death at his heart, this statue slowly bowed its head as if in recognition of a gallant fight.

Perhaps it was the sorrowful acceptance of a bitter ending.

7th July

Again upon the sea.

This time for Persia, bearing our wounded and the ashes of the dead; those of the natives are reposing beneath the Great Temple.

The skull of the last Mehrikan I shall present to the museum at Teheran.

(9,803 words)

Text 2: Red Rising (2014)

by Pierce Brown

Tasks

Pre-tasks connected with Red Rising:
Elon Musk: going to Mars.

To access the data needed for these tasks (indicated by the **underlined, bold words**), use Klett-Online code yww53kb (see page 8), or the Klett Augmented app accessible via page 59.

1. Find out about **Elon Musk's Vision of the Future**. Start by taking a look at a website, then
2. Watch a short video of **how Elon Musk plans to reach Mars.**
3. You can then watch **the full presentation** (just over one hour long!), or just take a look at the **slides (downloadable PDF)**

Red Rising: Background Information

Red Rising is the only one of our three sci-fi texts which is set on an another planet – Mars.

Darrow is a Red, a member of the lowest caste in the color-coded society of the future. Like all his fellow Reds, he works all day every day in the mines deep under the surface of Mars, believing that he and his people are making the planet livable for future generations.

Soon he discovers that humanity already reached the surface generations ago. Vast cities and sprawling parks spread across the planet. Darrow—and Reds like him—are nothing more than slaves to a decadent ruling class.

Inspired by a longing for justice, and driven by the memory of lost love, Darrow sacrifices everything to infiltrate the legendary Institute, a proving ground for the dominant Gold caste, where the next generation of humanity's overlords struggle for power. He will be forced to compete for his life and the very future of civilization against the best and most brutal of Society's ruling class. There, he will stop at nothing to bring down his enemies – even if it means he has to become one of them to do so.

We have two extracts from the book. The first is from the introduction, or preface. The second piece is from near the beginning of the story (pages 29 to 50 of the original). It consists of Chapters 4, 5 and 6, called respectively "The Gift", "The First Song" and "The Martyr".

1. PREFACE

I would have lived in peace. But my enemies brought me war.

I watch twelve hundred of their strongest sons and daughters. Listening to a pitiless Golden man speak between great marble pillars. Listening to the beast who brought the flame that gnaws at my heart.

"All men are *not* created equal," he declares. Tall, imperious, an eagle of a man. "The weak have deceived you. They would say the meek should inherit the Earth. That the strong should nurture the gentle. This is the Noble Lie of Demokracy. The cancer that poisoned mankind."

His eyes pierce the gathered students. "You and I are Gold. We are the end of the evolutionary line. We tower above the flesh heap of man, shepherding the lesser Colors. You have inherited this legacy," he pauses, studying faces in the assembly. "But it is not free".

"Power must be claimed. Wealth won. Rule, dominion, empire purchased with blood. You scarless children deserve nothing. You do not know pain. You do not know what your forefathers sacrificed to place you on these heights. But soon, you will. Soon, we will teach you why Gold rules mankind. And I promise, of those among you, only those fit for power will survive."

But I am no Gold. I am a Red.

He thinks men like me weak. He thinks me dumb, feeble, subhuman. I was not raised in palaces. I did not ride horses through meadows and eat meals of hummingbird tongues. I was forged in

5 **gnaw** [nɑː] bite – 7 **imperious** dictatorial, arrogant – 15 **legacy** inheritance, birthright

the bowels of this hard world. Sharpened by hate. Strengthened by love.

He is wrong.

None of them will survive.

[. . .]

CHAPTER 4. THE GIFT

As the Laurel-wreathed boxes come down to Gamma, I think about how clever it really is. They won't let us win the Laurel. They don't care that the math doesn't work. They don't care that the young scream in protest and the old moan their same tired wisdoms. This is just a demonstration of their power. It is their power. They decide the winner. A game of merit won by birth. It keeps the hierarchy in place. It keeps us striving, but never conspiring.

Yet despite the disappointment, some part of us doesn't blame the Society. We blame Gamma, who receives the gifts. A man's only got so much hate, I suppose. And when he sees his children's ribs through their shirts while his neighbors line their bellies with meat stews and sugared tarts, it's hard for him to hate anyone but them. You think they'd share. They don't.

My uncle shrugs at me and others are red and mad. Loran looks like he might attack the Tinpots or the Gammas. But Eo doesn't let me boil in it. She doesn't let my knuckles turn white as I clench my fists in fury. She knows the temper I have inside me better even than my own mother, and she knows how to drain the rage before it rises. My mother smiles softly as she watches Eo take me by the arm. How she loves my wife.

---

7 **laurel-wreathed** [riːθt] **box** *Kasten mit einem Lorbeerkranz versehen bzw. verziert* – 7 **Gamma** name of competing mining clan – 8 **Laurel** reward given to clan which mines the most helium-3 – 21 **Tinpots** slang for supervisors in higher "Gray" class

“Dance with me,” Eo whispers. She shouts for the zithers to get going and the drums to get rolling. No doubt she’s pissin’ fire. She hates the Society more than I do. But this is why I love my wife.

Soon the fast zither music swells and the old men slap their hands on tables. The layered skirts fly. Feet tap and shuffle. And I grasp my wife as the clans flow in dance throughout the square to join us. We sweat and we laugh and try to forget the anger. We grew together, and now are grown. In her eyes, I see my heart. In her breath, I hear my soul. She is my land. She is my kin. My love.

She pulls me away with laughter. We wend our way through the crowd to be alone. Yet she does not stop when we are free. She guides me along metal walkways and low, dark ceilings to the old tunnels, to the Webbery, where the women toil. It is between shifts.

“Where are we going exactly ?” I ask.

“If you remember, I have gifts for you. And if you apologize for your own gift going flat, I’ll smack you in the gob.

Seeing a bloody-red haemanthus bulb peeking out from the wall, I snatch it up and hand it to her. “My gift,” I said. “I did intend to surprise you.”

She giggles. “Well then. This inner half is mine. This outer half is yours. No! Don’t pull at it. I’m keeping your half.” I smell the haemanthus in her hand. It stinks like rust and Mother’s meager stews.

Inside the Webbery, thigh-thick spiderworms of brown and black fur, with long skeletal legs, knit silk around us. They crawl along the girders, thin legs disproportionate to their corpulent abdomens. Eo leads me into the Webbery’s highest level. The old metal girders are laced with silk. I shiver in looking at the creatures above and below; pitvipers I understand, spiderworms I do not. The Society’s Carvers

---

16 **gob** *sl for* mouth – 17 **haemanthus** *Blutblume* – 26 **girder** large beam *usu* made of iron or steel – 26 **corpulent** fat, large

made the creatures. Laughing, Eo guides me to a wall and pulls back a thick curtain of webbing, revealing a rusted metal duct.

“Ventilation,” she says. “Mortar on the walls gave way to reveal it about a week ago. An old tube too.”

“Eo, they’ll lash us if they find us. We’re not allowed…”

“I’m not going to let them ruin this gift too.” She kisses me on the nose. “Come on, Helldiver. There’s not even a molten drill in this tunnel.”

I follow her through a long series of turns in the small shaft till we exit out a grate into a world of inhuman sounds. A buzz murmurs in the darkness. She takes my hand. It’s the only familiar thing.

“What is that?” I ask of the sound.

“Animals,” she says, and leads me into the strange night. Something soft is beneath my feet. I nervously let her pull me forward. Grass. Trees. Darrow, trees. We’re in a forest.”

The scent of flowers. Then lights in the darkness. Flickering animals with green abdomens flutter through the black. Great bugs with iridescent wings rise from the shadows. They pulse with color and life. My breath catches and Eo laughs as a butterfly passes so close I can touch it.

They’re in our songs, all these things, but we’ve only ever seen them on the HC. Their colors are unlike any I could believe. My eyes have seen nothing but soil, the flare of the drill, Reds, and the gray of concrete and metal. The HC has been the window through which I’ve seen color. But this is a different spectacle.

The colors of the floating animals scald my eyes. I shiver and laugh and reach out and touch the creatures floating before me in the darkness. A child again, I cup them and look up at the room’s clear ceiling. It is a transparent bubble that peers at the sky.

---

18 **iridescent** [ˌɪrɪˈdɪsənt] glowing, shining – 22 **HC** *(abb)* holoCan, cube with TV screens on four sides

Sky. Once it was just a word.

I cannot see Mars's face, but I can see its view. Stars glow soft and graceful in the slick black sky, like the lights that dangle above our township. Eo looks as though she could join them. Her face is aglow as she watches me, laughing as I fall to my knees and suck in the scent of the grass. It is a strange smell, sweet and nostalgic, though I have no memories of grass. As the animals buzz near in the brush, in the trees, I pull her down, I kiss her with my eyes open for the first time. The trees and their leaves sway gently from the air that comes through the vents. And I drink the sounds, the smells, the sight as my wife and I make love in a bed of grass beneath a roof of stars.

"That is Andromeda Galaxy," she tells me later as we lie on our backs. The animals make chirping noises in the darkness. The sky above me is a frightening thing. If I stare too intently, I forget gravity's pull and feel as though I am going to fall into it. Shivers trickle down my spine. I am a creature of nooks and tunnels and shafts. The mine is my home, and part of me wants to run to safety, run from this alien room of living things and vast spaces.

Eo rolls to look at me and traces the steam scars that run like rivers down my chest. Farther down she'd find scars from the pitviper along my belly. "Mum used to tell me stories of Andromeda. She'd draw with inks given to her by that Tinpot, Bridge. He always liked her, you know."

As we lie together, she takes a deep breath and I know she has planned something, saved something to talk about in this moment. This place is leverage.

"You won the Laurel, we all know," she says to me.

"You needn't coddle me. I'm not angry any longer. It doesn't matter," I say. "After seeing this, none of that matters."

---

6 **nostalgic** longing for the past, sentimental – 27 **leverage** influence, sway

"What are you talking about?" she asks sharply. "It matters more than ever. You won the Laurel, but they didn't let you keep it."

"It doesn't matter. This place ..."

"This place exists, but they don't let us come here, Darrow. The Grays must use it for themselves. They don't share."

"Why should they?" I ask, confused.

"Because we made it. Because it's ours!"

"Is it?" The thought is foreign. All I possess is my family and myself. Everything else is the Society's. We didn't spend the money to send the pioneers here. Without them, we'd be on the dying Earth like the rest of humanity.

"Darrow! Are you so Red that you don't see what they've done to us?"

"Watch your tone," I say tightly.

Her jaw flexes. I'm sorry, it's just we *are* in chains, Darrow. We are not colonists. Well, sure we are. But it's more on the spot to call us slaves. We beg for food. Beg for Laurels like dogs begging for scraps from the master's table."

"You may be a slave," I snap. "But I am not. I don't beg. I earn. I am a Helldiver. I was born to sacrifice, to make Mars ready for man. There's a nobility to obedience ... ."

She throws up her hands. "A talking puppet, are you? Spitting out their bloodydamn lines. Your father had the right of it. He might not have been perfect, but he had the right of it." She grabs a clump of grass and tears it out of the ground. It seems like some sort of sacrilege.

"We have claim over this land, Darrow. Our sweat and blood watered this soil. Yet it belongs to the Golds, to the Society. How long has it been this way? A hundred, a hundred and fifty years of pioneers mining and dying? Our blood and their orders. We prepare

---

26 **sacrilege** ['sækrəlɪʤ] misuse of something holy or sacred – 28 **Golds** ruling class genetically modified to be physically superior

this land for Colors that have never shed sweat for us, Colors that sit in comfort on their thrones on distant Earth, Colors that have never been to Mars. Is that something to live for? I'll say it again, your father had the right of it."

I shake my head at her. "Eo, my father died before he was even twenty-five because he had the *right of it*."

"Your father was weak," she mutters.

"What the bloodydamn is that supposed to mean?" Blood rises into my face.

"It means he had too much restraint. It means your father had the right dream but died because he would not fight to make it real," she says sharply.

"He had a family to protect!"

"He was still weaker than you."

"*Careful*," I hiss.

"Careful? This from *Darrow*, the mad Helldiver of Lykos?" She laughs patronizingly. "Your father was born careful, obedient. But were you? I didn't think so when I married you. The others say you are like a machine, because they think you know no fear. They're blind. They don't see how fear binds you."

She traces the haemanthus blossom along my collarbone in a sudden show of tenderness. She is a creature of moods. The flower is the same color as the wedding band on her finger.

I roll on an elbow to face her. "Spit it out. What do you want?

"Do you know why I love you, Helldiver?" she asks.

"Because of my sense of humor."

She laughs dryly. "Because you *thought* you could win the Laurel. Kieran told me how you burned yourself today."

---

16 **Lykos** name of their underground mining colony – 28 **how you burned yourself today** In the previous chapter, deep in the mines, Darrow left the safety of his drill to scan for a potential life-threatening gas pocket. Climbing back up, his foot got stuck. While freeing himself his hand touched the very hot drill and was burned.

I sigh. "The rat. Always jabbering. Thought that's what younger brothers were supposed to do, not elder."

"Kieran was frightened, Darrow. Not *for* you, like you might be thinking. He was frightened *of* you, because he can't do what you did. Boy wouldn't even think it."

She always talks circles around me. I hate the abstracts she lives for.

"So you love me because you believe that I think there are things worth the risk?" I puzzle out. "Or because I'm ambitious?

"Because you've a brain," she teases.

She makes me ask it again. "What do you want me to do, Eo?"

"Act. I want you to use your gifts for your father's dream. You see how people watch you, take their cues from you. I want you to think owning this land, our land, is worth the risk."

"How much a risk?"

"Your life. My life."

I scoff. "You're that eager to be rid of me?"

"Speak and they will listen," she urges. "It is that bloody simple. All ears yearn for a voice to lead them through darkness."

"Grand, so I'll hang with a troop. I am my father's son."

"You won't hang."

I laugh too harshly. "So certain a wife I have. I'll hang."

"You're not meant to be a martyr." Sighing, she lies back in disappointment. "You wouldn't see the point to it."

"Oh? Well then, tell me, Eo. What is the point to dying? I'm only a martyr's son. So tell me what that man accomplished by robbing me of a father. Tell me what good comes of all that *bloodydamn* sadness. Tell me why it's better I learned to dance from my uncle than my father." I go on. "Did his death put food on your table? Did it make any of our lives any better? Dying for a cause doesn't do a bloodydamn thing. It just robbed us of his laughter." I feel the tears burning my eye. "It just stole away a father and a husband. So what if life isn't fair? If we have family, that is all that should matter."

She licks her lips and takes her time in replying.

"Death isn't empty like you say it is. Emptiness is life without freedom, Darrow. Emptiness is living chained by fear, fear of loss, of death. I say we break those chains. Break the chains of fear and you break the chains that bind us to the Golds, to the Society. Could you imagine it? Mars could be ours. It could belong to the colonists who slaved here, died here." Her face is easier to see as night fades through the clear roof. It is alive, on fire. "If you led the others to freedom. The things you could do, Darrow. The things you could make happen." She pauses and I see her eyes are glistening. "It chills me. You have been given so, so much, but you set your sights so low."

"You repeat the same damn points," I say bitterly. "You think a dream is worth dying for. I say it isn't. You say it's better to die on your feet. I say it's better to live on our knees."

"You're not even living!" she snaps. "We are machine men with machine minds, machine lives … ."

"And machine hearts?" I ask. "That's what I am?"

"Darrow …"

"What do you live for?" I ask her suddenly. "Is it for me? Is it for family and love? Or is it for some dream?"

"It's not just *some* dream, Darrow. I live for *the* dream that my children will be born free. That they will be what they like. That they will own the land their *father* gave them."

"I live for you," I say sadly.

She kisses my cheek. "Then you must live for more."

There's a long, terrible silence that stretches between us. She does not understand how her words wrench my heart, how she can twist me so easily. Because she does not love me like I love her. Her mind is too high. Mine too low. Am I not enough for her?

"You said you had another gift for me?" I say, changing the subject.

She shakes her head. "Some other time. The sun rises. Watch it with me once, at least."

We lie in silence and watch light slip into the sky as though it were a tide made from fire. It is unlike anything I could have dreamed of. I can't stop the tears that well in the corners of my eyes as the world beyond turns to light and the greens and browns and yellows of the trees in the room are revealed. It is beauty. It is a dream.

I am silent as we return to the grimness of the gray ducts. The tears linger in my eyes and as the majesty of what I saw fades; I wonder what Eo wants of me. Does she want me to take my slingBlade and start a rebellion? I would die. My family would die. She would die, and nothing would make me risk her. She knows that.

I am puzzling out what her other gift may be when we exit the ducts for the Webbery. I roll first from the duct and extend a hand back to her when I hear a voice. It is accented, oily, from Earth.

"Reds in our gardens," it oozes. "Ain't that a thing."

5. THE FIRST SONG

Ugly Dan stands with three Tinpots. Their thumpers perch crackling in their hands. Two of the men lean on the metal rails of the Webbery's girders. Behind them, the women of Mu and Upsilon wrap silk from the worms around long silver poles. They shake their heads insistently at me, as if telling me not to be foolish. We've gone beyond the permitted zones. This will mean a flogging, but if I resist, it will mean death. They will kill Eo and they will kill me.

"Darrow … ," Eo murmurs.

I set myself between Eo and the Tinpots, but I don't fight. I won't let us die for a simple glimpse of the stars. I put my hands out to let them know I will surrender.

---

10 **slingBlade** curved sword used to cut off caught limbs in mines – 18 **thumper** type of electrical weapon

"Helldivers," Ugly Dan chuckles to the others. "The toughest ant is yet but an ant." He swings his thumper into my stomach. It's like being bitten by a viper and kicked by a boot. I fall gasping, hands on the metal grate. Electricity slithers through my veins. I taste the bile rising in my throat. "Take a swing, Helldiver," Dan coos. He drops one of the thumpers in front of me. "Please. Take a swing. Won't be any consequences. Just some fun between the boys. Take a piggin' swing."

"Do it, Darrow!" Eo shouts.

I'm not a fool. I thrust my hands up in surrender and Dan sighs in disappointment as he clacks the magnetic manacles around my wrists. What would Eo have had me do? She curses at them as they lock her arms together and drag us away through the Webbery to the cells. This will mean the lash. But it will be just the lash because I did not pick up the thumper, because I did not listen to Eo.

It's three days in a cell in the Pot before I see Eo again. Bridge, one of the old, kinder Tinpots, takes us out together; he lets us touch. I wonder if she'll spit at me, curse me for my impotence. But she only grips my fingers and brings her lips to mine.

"Darrow." Her lips brush my ear. The breath is warm, the lips cracked and trembling. She's frail as she hugs me – a little girl, all wire wrapped in pale skin. Her knees wobble and she shudders against me. The warmth I saw in her face as we watched the sun rise has fled and left her like a faded memory. But I hardly see anything but her eyes and her hair. I wrap my arms around her and hear the muttering of the crowded Common. The faces of our kin and clan stare at us as we stand at the edge of the gallows, where they will flog us. I feel like a child under their stares, under the yellowish lights.

---

18 **impotence** weakness, powerlessness

It's like a dream when Eo tells me she loves me. Her hand lingers on mine. But there's something strange to her eyes. They should only whip her, yet her words are final, her eyes sad but not afraid. I see her making a goodbye. A nightmare is coming to my heart. I can feel it like a nail dragged along the bones of my spine as she murmurs an epigram in my ear. "Break the chains, my love."

And then I am jerked away from her by my hair. Tears stream down her face. They are for me, though I do not yet understand why. I cannot think. The world is swimming. I am drowning. Rough hands shove me to my knees, then jerk me up. I've never heard the Common so quiet. The shuffling of my captors' feet echoes as they move me around.

The Tinpots fit me into my Helldiver frysuit. Its acrid smell makes me think I am safe, I am in control. I am not. I'm dragged away from her into the very center of the Common and tossed at the edge of the gallows. The metal stairs are rusted and stained. I grip them with my hands and look to the top of the gallows. Twenty-four of the headTalks each have a cord of leather. They wait for me atop the platform.

"Oh, the horror of such occasions as this, my friends," Magisrate Podginus cries. His copper gravBoots hum above me as he floats through the air. "Oh, how the ties that bind us are stretched when one decides to break the laws which protect us all.

"Even the youngest, even the best, are subject to Law. To Order! Without these we would be animals! Without obedience, without discipline, there would be no colonies! And those few colonies there are would be torn asunder by disorder! Man would be confined to Earth. Man would wallow forevermore on that planet until the end of days. But Order! Discipline! Law! These are the things which

---

6 **epigram** words of wisdom, saying – 18 **headTalk** leader of mining crew – 27 **asunder** apart, up

empower our race. Cursed is the creature who breaks with these compacts."

The speech is more eloquent than usual. Podginus is trying to impress his intelligence upon someone. I look up from the stairs and see a sight I did not ever think to see with my own two eyes. It stings to look at him, to drink in the radiance of his hair, of his Sigils. I see a Gold. In this drab place, he is what I imagine angels would be like. Cloaked in gold and black. Wrapped in the sun. A lion roaring upon his breast.

His face is older, severe, and pure with power. His hair shines, combed back against his head. Neither a smile nor a frown mark his thin lips, and the only line I see is that of a scar, which runs along his right cheekbone.

I've learned from the HC that such a scar is borne only by the finest of the Golds. The Peerless Scarred, they call them – men and women of the ruling Color who have graduated from the Institute, where they learn the secrets that will permit mankind to one day colonize all the planets of the Solar System.

He does not speak to us. He speaks to another Gold, one tall and thin, so thin I thought it a woman at first. Without a scar, the man's face is coated with strange paste to bring out the color of his cheeks and cover the lines on his face. His lips shine. And his hair glistens in a way his master's does not. He is a grotesque thing to look upon. He thinks so of us. He sniffs the air, contemptuous. The older Gold speaks to him softly and not to us.

And why should he speak to us? We are not worthy of a Gold's words. I scarcely want to look at him. I feel like I dirty his gold and black finery with my red eyes. Shame creeps upon me and then I realize why.

---

23 **grotesque** disgusting, deformed

His is a face I know. It is a face every man and woman of the colonies would know. Besides Octavia au Lune, this is the most famous face on Mars – that of Nero au Augustus. The ArchGovernor of Mars has come to see me flogged, and he has brought a retinue. Two Crows (Obsidians to be technic) float quietly behind him. Their skull helmets suit their Color. I was born to mine the earth. They were born to kill men. More than two feet taller than I. Eight fingers on each massive hand. They breed them for war, and watching them is like watching the coldblooded pitvipers who infest our mines. Reptiles both.

There are a dozen others in his retinue, including another, slighter Gold who seems his apprentice. He's even more beautiful than the ArchGovernor and he appears to dislike the thin, womanish Gold. And there is an HC camera crew of Greens, tiny creatures compared with the Crows. Their hair is dark. Not green like their eyes. And the Sigils on their hands. Frenetic excitement shimmers in those eyes. It's not often they have Helldivers to make into an example, so they make a spectacle of me. I wonder how many other mining colonies are watching. All of them, if the ArchGovernor is here.

They make a show of stripping away the frysuit they only just dressed me in. I see myself on the HC display above, see my wedding band dangling from the cord around my neck. I look younger than I feel, thinner. They jerk me up the stairs and bend me over a metal box beside the noose where my father hung. I shiver as they lay me across the cold steel and tighten my hands in restraints. I smell the synthleather of the lashes, hear one of the headTalks cough.

"Forevermore, let justice be done," Podginus says.

Then the lashes come. Forty-eight in all. They aren't soft, not even my uncle's. They can't be. The lashes bite and wail into my flesh, making a strange keening noise as they arch through the air.

---

4 retinue ['ret̬ənu:] group of employees, advisors and assistants – **16 sigil** symbol, sign

Music of terror. I can barely see by the end of it. I pass out twice, and each time I wake I wonder if you can see my spine on the HC.

It's a show, all a show of their power. They let the Tinpot, Ugly Dan, act sympathetic, as though he pities me. He whispers encouragement in my ear loud enough for the cameras. And when the last lash slashes my back, he steps in as if to stop another from coming down. Subconsciously; I think he saves me. I'm thankful. I want to kiss him. He is salvation. But I know I've had my forty-eight.

Then they are dragging me to the side. They leave my blood. I'm sure I screamed, sure I shamed myself. I hear them bring out my wife.

"Even the young, even the beautiful cannot escape justice. It is for all the Colors that we preserve Order, Justice. Without, we would find anarchy. Without Obedience, chaos! Man would perish upon the irradiated sands of Earth. He would drink from the blasted seas. There must be unity. Forevermore, let justice be done."

MineMagistrate Podginus's words ring hollow.

No one is offended that I'm bloody and beaten. But when Eo is dragged atop the gallows, there are cries. There are curses. Even now she is beautiful, even drained of the light I saw in her three days ago. Even as she sees me and lets the tears come down her face, she is an angel.

All this for a little adventure. All this for a night under the stars with the man she loves. Yet she is calm. If there is fear, it is in me, because I feel a strangeness in the air. Her skin prickles as they lay her across the cold box. She flinches. I wish my blood had warmed it better for her.

When they whip Eo, I try not to watch. But it hurts more to abandon her. Her eyes find mine. They shine like rubies, twitch

---

16 **irradiate** [ɪˈreɪdieɪt] expose to radiation

every time the lash falls. *Soon this will be over, my love. Soon we will go back to life. Just last the lash and we get everything back.* But can she even take so many lashes?

"End it," I say to the Tinpot beside me. "End it!" I beg of him. "I'll do anything. I'll obey. I'll take her lashes. Just end it, you bloody-damn bastards! End it!"

The ArchGovernor looks down at me, but his face is golden, poreless, and without care. I am nothing but the bloodiest of ants. My sacrifice will impress him. He'll feel compassion if I abase myself, if I throw myself into the fire for love. He'll feel pity. This is how the stories go.

"Your Excellency, give me her punishment!" I plead. "Please!" I beg because in my wife's eyes I see something that terrifies me. I see fight in her as they streak her back bloody. I see anger building inside her. There is a reason she is not afraid.

"*No. No. No,*" I plead to her. "*No, Eo. Please, no!*"

"Gag that wretched thing! He prickles the ArchGovernor's ears," Podginus orders. Bridge forces a knot of stone into my mouth. I gag and cry.

As the thirteenth lash falls, as I mumble for her not to do it, Eo stares into my eyes one last moment and then she begins her song. It is a quiet sound, a mournful sound, like the song the deep mines whisper as wind moves in the abandoned shafts. It is the song of death and lament, the song that is forbidden. The song I have only heard once before.

For this, they will kill her.

Her voice is soft and true, never as beautiful as she. It echoes across the Common, rising up like a Siren's unearthly call. The lashes pause. The headTalks shiver. Even the Tinpots sadly shake their heads when they place the words. Few men truly like seeing beauty burn.

Podginus glances embarrassedly over at ArchGovernor Augustus, who descends on golden gravBoots to watch more closely. His shining hair glistens against his noble brow. High cheekbones catch the light. Those golden eyes examine my wife as though a worm had suddenly sprouted a butterfly's wings. His scar curves as he speaks with a voice dripping power.

"Let her sing," he says to Podginus, not bothering to hide his fascination.

"But, my lord …"

"No animal but man throws themselves willingly into the flames, Copper. Relish the sight. You'll not see it again." To his camera crew: "Continue recording. We will edit out the parts we find intolerable."

How futile his words make her sacrifice seem.

But never has Eo been more beautiful to me than in that moment. In the face of cold power, she is fire. This is the girl who danced through the smoky tav with a mane of red. This is the girl who wove me a wedding band of her own hair. This is the girl who chooses to die for a song of death.

My love, my love
Remember the cries
When winter died for spring skies
They roared and roared
But we grabbed our seed
And sowed a song
Against their greed

And
Down in the vale
Hear the reaper swing, the reaper swing
the reaper swing
Down in the vale
Hear the reaper sing
A tale of winter done

My son, my son
Remember the chains
When gold ruled with iron reins
We roared and roared
And twisted and screamed
For ours, a vale
of better dreams

As her voice finally swells and the song runs out of words, I know I have lost her. She becomes something more important; and she was right, I do not understand.

"A quaint tune. But is that all you have?" the ArchGovernor asks her when she is through. He looks at her but he speaks loudly, to the crowd, to those who will watch in the other colonies. His entourage chuckles at Eo's weapon, a song. What is a song but notes unto the air? Useless as a match in a storm against his power. He shames us. "Do any of you wish to join her in song? I implore you, bold Reds of .. ." He looks to his assistant, who mouths the name. "...Lykos, join her now if you wish."

I can barely breathe past the stone. It chips my molars. Tears stream down my face. No voices rise from the crowd. I see my mother trembling with anger. Kieran clutches his wife close. Narol stares at the ground. Loran weeps. They are all here, all quiet. All afraid.

"Alas, Your Excellency, we find the girl alone in her zealotry," Podginus declares. Eo has eyes only for me. "Tis clear her opinion is an outlier's, an outcast's. Mayhaps we should proceed?"

"Yes," the ArchGovernor says idly. "I have an appointment with Arcos. Hang the rusty bitch lest she continue to howl."

24 zealotry ['zelətri] radicalism, extremism

6. THE MARTYR

For Eo, I do not react. I am anger. I am hatred. Everything. But I hold her gaze even as they take her away and fit the noose around her neck. I look up at Bridge and he quietly takes the gag from my mouth. My teeth will never be the same. Tears build in the Tinpot's eyes. I leave him and stumble numbly to the bottom of the scaffold so Eo can see me as she dies. This is her choice. I will be with her to the end. My hands shake. Sobs come from the crowd behind me.

"The last words, to whom will you speak them before justice is done?" Podginus asks her. He drips sympathy for the camera.

I ready for her to say my name, but she does not. Her eyes never leave mine, but she calls her sister out. "Dio." The word trembles in the air. She is frightened now. I do not react as Dio climbs the scaffold stairs; I do not understand, but I will not be jealous. This is not about me. I love her. And her choice is made. I do not understand, but I will not let her die knowing anything but my love.

Ugly Dan has to help Dio climb the gallows; she's stumbling and senseless as she leans close to her sister. Whatever is said, I do not hear; but Dio lets loose a moan that will haunt me forever. She looks at me as she weeps. What did my wife tell her? Women are crying. Men wipe their eyes. They have to stun Dio to pull her away, but she clings to Eo's feet, weeping. There is a nod from the ArchGovernor, though he doesn't even care enough to watch as, like my father, Eo is hanged.

"*Live for more*," she mouths to me. She reaches into her pocket and pulls out the haemanthus I gave her. It is smashed and flat. Then loudly she screams to all those gathered, "Break the chains!"

The trapdoor beneath her feet opens. She falls, and for one moment, her hair hangs suspended about her head, a flourish of red. Then her feet scramble at air and she falls. Her slim throat gags. Eyes open so wide. If only I could save her from this. If only I could protect her; but the world is cold and hard to me. It does not bend as I wish it to bend. I am weak. I watch my wife die and my haemanthus fall from her hand. The camera records it all. I rush forward to kiss her ankle. I cradle her legs. I will not let her suffer.

On Mars there is not much gravity, so you have to pull the feet to break the neck. They let the loved ones do it.

Soon, there is no sound, not even the creaking of the rope.

My wife is too light.

She was only just a girl.

Then the thumping of the Fading Dirge begins. Fists on chests. Thousands. Fast, like a racing heartbeat. Slower. A beat a second. A beat every five. Every ten. Then never again, and the mournful mass fades away like dust held in the palm as the old tunnels wail with deep winds.

And the Golds, they fly away.

Eo's father, Loran, and Kieran sit by my door through the night. They say they are there to keep me company. But they are there to guard me, to ensure I do not die. I want to die. Mother dresses my wound with silk my sister, Leanna, stole from the Webbery.

"Keep the nervenucleic dry, or you will scar."

What are scars? How little they matter. Eo will not see them, so why should I care? She will not run her hand along my back. She will never kiss my wounds.

She is gone.

I lie in our bed on my back so I can feel the pain and forget my wife. But I cannot forget. She hangs even now. In the morning, I will pass her on the way to the mines. Soon she will stink and soon she will rot. My beautiful wife shone too bright to live long. I still feel her neck cracking against my hands; they tremble now in the night.

There is a hidden tunnel I carved in my bedroom long ago in the rock so I could sneak out as a child. I use it now. I leave out the secret path, climbing stealthily down from my home, so my kin never see me slip away in the low light.

It is quiet in the township. Quiet except for the HC, which makes my wife die to a soundtrack. They intended to show the futility of disobedience. And they succeed in that, but there is something else in the video. They show my flogging, and Eo's, and they play her song throughout. And as she dies, they play it again, which seems to give the video the wrong effect. Even if she were not my wife, I see a martyr, a young girl's pretty song silenced by the rope of cruel men.

Then the HC flashes black for several moments. It has never gone to black before. And Octavia au Lune comes back on with the same old message. It almost seems as though someone has hacked into the broadcast, because my wife flickers onto the giant screen again.

"Break the chains!" she cries. Then she's gone and the screen is black. It crackles. The image comes back. She cries it again. Black once more. Standard programming goes up, then it cuts to her screaming one last time and then there's me pulling her legs. Then static.

The streets are quiet as I make my way to the Common. The nightshift will be returning soon. Then I hear a noise and a man steps into the street in front of me. My uncle's face leers at me from the shadows. A single bulb hangs over his head, illuminating the flask in his hand and his tattered red shirt.

"You are your father's son, little bastard. Stupid and vain."

My hands clench. "Come to stop me, Uncle?"

He grunts. "Couldn't stop your father from killing his bloody self. And he was a better bloodyman than you. More restraint in him."

I step forward. "I don't need your permission."

"Nay, you little squabber, you don't." He runs a hand through his hair. "Don't do what you're gonna do, though. It'll break your

---

2 **futility** pointlessness, uselessness – 21 **leer** stare at sb *usu* in mean or unpleasant way

mother; you might think she didn't know you'd slip out. She did. Told me so. Said you were gonna go die like my brother, like your girl."

"If Mother knew, she would have stopped me."

"Nah. She lets us men make our own mistakes. But this ain't what your girl would've wanted."

I point a finger at my uncle. "You don't know a thing. Not a thing about what she wanted." Eo said I wouldn't understand being a martyr. I will show her I do.

"Righto," he says with a shrug. "I'll walk with you, then, since your head is full of rocks." He chuckles. "We Lambdas do love the noose."

He tosses me his flask and I fall into tentative step beside him.

"I tried to talk your father out of his little protest, you know. Told him words and dance mean as much as dust. Tried squaring up with him. I squabbed that one up. He laid me down cold." He throws a slow right. "Comes a time in life when you know a man has his mind set and it's an insult to gainsay."

I drink from his flask and hand it back. The swill tastes strange and thicker than usual. Strange. He makes me finish the flask.

"Your's set?" he asks, tapping his head. "Course it is. I forget, I taught you how to dance."

"Stubborn as a pitviper, wasn't that how you put it?" I say quietly, allowing a little smile.

I walk in silence for a moment with my uncle. He puts a hand on my shoulder. A sob wants to come out of my chest. I swallow it.

"She left me," I whisper. "Just left me."

"Musta had a reason. Not a dumb girl, that one."

The tears come as I enter the Common. My uncle takes me in a one-armed hug and kisses the crown of my head. It's all he can offer.

---

19 **swill** alcoholic drink

He's not a man made for affection. His face is pale and ghostly. Thirty-five and so old, so tired. A scar twists his upper lip. Gray streaks his thick hair.

"Tell them hello for me in the vale," he says into my ear, his beard coarse against my neck. "Give my brothers a toast and my wife a kiss, specially Dancer."

"Dancer?"

"You'll know him. And if you see your gramp and gran, tell them we still dance for them. They won't be long alone." He walks away, then pauses and without turning says, "Break the chains. Hear?"

"Hear."

He leaves me there in the Common with my swaying wife. I know the cameras watch me from the can as I walk up the gallows. It is metal, so the stairs don't creak. She hangs like a doll. Her face is pale as chalk and her hair shifts slightly as the ventilators rasp above.

When the rope has been cut with the slingBlade I stole from the mines, I grab its frayed end and lower her down gently. I take my wife in my arms and together wend our way from the square to the Webbery. A nightshift is working their final hours. The women watch in silence as I carry Eo to the ventilation duct. There I see Leanna, my sister. Tall and quiet like my mother, she watches me with hard eyes, but she does nothing. None of the women do. They will not gossip about where my wife is buried. They will not speak, not even for the chocolate given to spies. Only five souls have been buried in three generations – someone always hangs for it.

This is the ultimate act of love. Eo's silent requiem.

Women begin to cry, and as I pass they reach to touch Eo's face, to touch mine and help me open the ventilation duct. I drag my wife through the tight metal space, taking her to where we made love beneath the stars, where she told me her plans and I did not listen.

---

26 **requiem** act of remembrance in honor of sacrifice or death

I hold her lifeless body and hope her soul sees me in a place where we were happy.

I dig a hole near the base of a tree. My hands, covered with the dirt of our land, are red like her hair as I take her hand and kiss her wedding band. I place the outer bulb of the haemanthus atop her heart and take the inner and put it near my own. Then I kiss her lips and bury her. But I sob before I can finish. I uncover her face and kiss her again and hold my body to hers till I see a red sun rising through the artificial bubbleroof. The colors of the place scald my eyes and I cannot stop my tears. When I pull away, I see my headband poking from her pocket. She made it for me to take my sweat. I give it my tears now and take it with me.

Kieran strikes me in the face when he sees me back in the township. Loran cannot speak, while Eo's father slumps against a wall. They think they failed me. I hear Eo's mother's cries. My mother says nothing as she makes me a meal. I don't feel well. It's hard to breathe. Leanna comes in late and helps her, kissing me on the head as I eat, lingering long enough to smell my hair. I must use one hand as I move the food from plate to mouth. My mother holds my other hand between her callused palms. She watches it instead of me, as though remembering when it was small and soft and wondering how it became so hard.

I finish the meal just as Ugly Dan comes. My mother does not leave the table as I'm pulled away. Her eyes stay fixed on where my hand lay. I think she believes if she does not look up, this will not happen. Even she can only bear so much.

They will hang me before a full assembly at nine in the morning. I'm dizzy for some reason. My heart feels funny, slow. I hear the ArchGovernor's words to my wife echo.

"Is that all your strength?"

My people sing, we dance, we love. That is our strength. But we also dig. And then we die. Seldom do we get to choose why. That choice is power. That choice has been our only weapon. But it is not enough.

They give me my last words. I call Dio up. Her eyes are bloodshot and swollen. She's a fragile thing, so unlike her sister.

"What were Eo's last words?" I ask her, though my mouth moves slowly, oddly.

She glances back to Mother, who finally followed but now shakes her head. There is something they are not telling me. Something they don't want me to know. A secret held back even though I am about to die.

"She said she loved you."

I don't believe her, but I smile and kiss her forehead. She can't handle more questions. And I'm dizzy. Hard to speak.

"I'll tell her you say hello."

I do not sing. I am made for other things.

My death is senseless. It is love.

But Eo was right, I don't understand this. This is not my victory. This is selfish. She told me to live for more. She wanted me to fight. But here I am, dying despite what she wanted. Giving up because of the pain.

I panic as suicides do when they realize their folly.

Too late.

I feel the door beneath me open. My body falls. Rope flays my neck. My spine creaks. Needles lance my lumbar. Kieran stumbles forward. Uncle Narol shoves him away. With a wink, he touches my feet and pulls.

I hope they do not bury me.

(8,077 words)

---

21 **folly** mistake, foolishness

Text 3: The Hunger Games (2008)

by Suzanne Collins

In "The Hunger Games" we have another post-apocalyptic vision of a future America.

Suzanne Collins was born in 1962. Her father was in the US military; he fought in Vietnam. Suzanne has said that as a child she thought a lot about war – especially about how it is reported. She grew up watching events on TV which were part of a war in which her father might be killed.

As an adult, the idea for The Hunger Games came to her while she was flipping between a TV reality show and reports of the Iraq War. "These two things came together in my mind in a very unsettling way", she has said.

Further inspiration came from Greek mythology. In the story of Theseus and the Minotaur, every year seven young men and seven young women from Athens were said to be sent to an underground labyrinth, where they were hunted and killed by the Minotaur, a mythical monster. Theseus is the battling hero.

Suzanne then thought about gladiators. There are three important elements to a gladiator story, she says: "One, a ruthless and all-powerful government which tolerates no dissent from the people; two, a fight to the death; and three, the fight should be popular entertainment for a cruel dictator and his friends.

And so the dystopian state of Panem formed in her mind.

---

20 **dissent** [dɪ'sent] resistance, disagreement

There are three extracts here:

1. ***The Reaping.*** *Near the beginning of the story, in Chapter 1, we read about the selection process of the young people who will represent the District in the Hunger Games. The story is narrated by the female protagonist, Katniss Everdeen.*
2. ***After the Hunger Games.*** *Chapters 26 and 27: the Games are over, what happens next?*
3. ***President Snow*** *(from the second novel, "Catching Fire") Back home in District 12, Katniss receives a VIP visit…*

Tasks

Pre-reading:
Watch the ***Hunger Games*** **movie trailer** (access it via Klett Online-Link yww53kb, or use the Klett Augmented app – scan via page 59).

Task: Describe Panem.

Extract 1: The Reaping

At one o'clock, we head for the square. Attendance is mandatory unless you are on death's door. This evening, officials will come around and check to see if this is the case. If not, you'll be imprisoned.

It's too bad, really, that they hold the reaping in the square — one of the few places in District 12 that can be pleasant. The square's surrounded by shops, and on public market days, especially if there's good weather, it has a holiday feel to it. But today, despite the bright banners hanging on the buildings, there's an air of grimness. The camera crews, perched like buzzards on rooftops, only add to the effect.

People file in silently and sign in. The reaping is a good opportunity for the Capitol to keep tabs on the population as well. Twelve- through eighteen-year-olds are herded into roped areas marked off by ages, the oldest in the front, the young ones, like Prim, toward the back. Family members line up around the perimeter, holding tightly to one another's hands. But there are others, too, who have no one they love at stake, or who no longer care, who slip among the crowd, taking bets on the two kids whose names will be drawn. Odds are given on their ages, whether they're Seam or merchant, if they will break down and weep. Most refuse dealing with the racketeers but carefully, carefully. These same people tend to be informers, and who hasn't broken the law? I could be shot on a daily basis for hunting, but the appetites of those in charge protect me. Not everyone can claim the same.

---

2 **to head for** to go quickly to – 2 **attendance is mandatory** people must be present – 5 **to be imprisoned** to be put into prison – 13 **to file in** to walk in a straight line in long queues – 14 **to keep tabs on** to check the number of and keep under observation – 15 **roped** *(adj) mit Seilen abgetrennt* – 19 **at stake** at risk, in peril

Anyway, Gale and I agree that if we have to choose between dying of hunger and a bullet in the head, the bullet would be much quicker.

The space gets tighter, more claustrophobic as people arrive. The square's quite large, but not enough to hold District 12's population of about eight thousand. Latecomers are directed to the adjacent streets, where they can watch the event on screens as it's televised live by the state.

I find myself standing in a clump of sixteens from the Seam. We all exchange terse nods then focus our attention on the temporary stage that is set up before the Justice Building. It holds three chairs, a podium, and two large glass balls, one for the boys and one for the girls. I stare at the paper slips in the girls' ball. Twenty of them have Katniss Everdeen written on them in careful handwriting.

Two of the three chairs fill with Madge's father, Mayor Undersee, who's a tall, balding man, and Effie Trinket, District 12's escort, fresh from the Capitol with her scary white grin, pinkish hair, and spring green suit. They murmur to each other and then look with concern at the empty seat.

Just as the town clock strikes two, the mayor steps up to the podium and begins to read. It's the same story every year. He tells of the history of Panem, the country that rose up out of the ashes of a place that was once called North America. He lists the disasters, the droughts, the storms, the fires, the encroaching seas that swallowed up so much of the land, the brutal war for what little sustenance remained. The result was Panem, a shining Capitol ringed by thirteen districts, which brought peace and prosperity to its citizens. Then came the Dark Days, the uprising of the districts

---

1 **Gale** Katniss's very close friend and hunting partner – 6 **adjacent** [ə'dʒeɪsənt] nearby, at the side – 9 **clump** *(inf)* group – 10 **nod** *kurzes Nicken mit dem Kopf* – 18 **suit** [su:t] *Anzug* – 18 **with concern at** worried, nervously – 24 **drought** [draʊt] hard time when no rain falls at all – 24 **to encroach** come nearer and bigger threateningly – 27 **prosperity** *Wohlstand*

against the Capitol. Twelve were defeated, the thirteenth obliterated. The Treaty of Treason gave us the new laws to guarantee peace and, as our yearly reminder that the Dark Days must never be repeated, it gave us the Hunger Games.

The rules of the Hunger Games are simple. In punishment for the uprising, each of the twelve districts must provide one girl and one boy, called tributes, to participate. The twenty-four tributes will be imprisoned in a vast outdoor arena that could hold anything from a burning desert to a frozen wasteland. Over a period of several weeks, the competitors must fight to the death. The last tribute standing wins.

Taking the kids from our districts, forcing them to kill one another while we watch — this is the Capitol's way of reminding us how totally we are at their mercy. How little chance we would stand of surviving another rebellion.

Whatever words they use, the real message is clear. "Look how we take your children and sacrifice them and there's nothing you can do. If you lift a finger, we will destroy every last one of you. Just as we did in District Thirteen."

To make it humiliating as well as torturous, the Capitol requires us to treat the Hunger Games as a festivity, a sporting event pitting every district against the others. The last tribute alive receives a life of ease back home, and their district will be showered with prizes, largely consisting of food. All year, the Capitol will show the winning district gifts of grain and oil and even delicacies like sugar while the rest of us battle starvation.

"It is both a time for repentance and a time for thanks," intones the mayor.

---

1 **to obliterate** eliminate – 6 **uprising** revolution, rebellion – 14 **to be at sb's mercy** to depend totally on sb, to be their slave – 20 **humiliating** *(adj) demütigend, erniedrigend* – 20 **torturous** *(adj) quälend* – 26 **starvation** extreme hunger – 27 **repentance** regret of wrongdoing *(Sühne)*

Then he reads the list of past District 12 victors. In seventy-four years, we have had exactly two. Only one is still alive. Haymitch Abernathy, a paunchy, middle-aged man, who at this moment appears hollering something unintelligible, staggers onto the stage, and falls into the third chair. He's drunk. Very. The crowd responds with its token applause, but he's confused and tries to give Effie Trinket a big hug, which she barely manages to fend off.

The mayor looks distressed. Since all of this is being televised, right now District 12 is the laughingstock of Panem, and he knows it. He quickly tries to pull the attention back to the reaping by introducing Effie Trinket.

Bright and bubbly as ever, Effie Trinket trots to the podium and gives her signature, "Happy Hunger Games! And may the odds be ever in your favor!" Her pink hair must be a wig because her curls have shifted slightly offcenter since her encounter with Haymitch. She goes on a bit about what an honor it is to be here, although everyone knows she's just aching to get bumped up to a better district where they have proper victors, not drunks who molest you in front of the entire nation.

Through the crowd, I spot Gale looking back at me with a ghost of a smile. As reapings go, this one at least has a slight entertainment factor. But suddenly I am thinking of Gale and his forty-two names in that big glass ball and how the odds are not in his favor. Not compared to a lot of the boys. And maybe he's thinking the same thing about me because his face darkens and he turns away. "But there are still thousands of slips," I wish I could whisper to him.

It's time for the drawing. Effie Trinket says as she always does, "Ladies first!" and crosses to the glass ball with the girls' names. She

---

4 **to holler** to shout around in an uncontrolled way – 4 **unintelligible** not understandable – 7 **to fend off** to escape – 14 **wig** *Perrücke* – 17 **to ache to do sth** to be very keen on sth, to want sth very much – 17 **to get bumped up to** *(inf)* to get promoted, transferred to a better place – 18 **to molest sb** to attack sb (*esp* a child) sexually *(belästigen)*

reaches in, digs her hand deep into the ball, and pulls out a slip of paper. The crowd draws in a collective breath and then you can hear a pin drop, and I'm feeling nauseous and so desperately hoping that it's not me, that it's not me, that it's not me.

Effie Trinket crosses back to the podium, smoothes the slip of paper, and reads out the name in a clear voice. And it's not me.

It's Primrose Everdeen.

Extract 2: After the Hunger Games have finished

Story update:

Upon hearing her sister Primrose's name called at the Reaping, Katniss immediately volunteers to take her place. She and Peeta, the boy who saved her from starving when they were young, then represent District 12 in the Hunger Games. Throughout the Games, Katniss must do whatever she can to gain sponsors and keep herself and Peeta alive, including kissing Peeta, in order to provide love interest in the hope that the audience and sponsors will support her and Peeta.

When, at the end, Katniss and Peeta are the two remaining survivors, the Gamemakers insist that one of them must die. However, instead of fighting each other, they threaten to both eat poisonous berries, which would destroy the whole point of the Games and displease the audience in the Capitol. The organisers thus allow them both to live.

At the end of Chapter 26, there is this conversation which takes place soon after the end of the Games between Katniss ("I") and Haymitch, who was her and Peeta's mentor and coach. In Chapter 27, Katniss is on TV, being interviewed by Caesar Flickerman in a live talk show.

"Listen up. You're in trouble. Word is the Capitol's furious about you showing them up in the arena. The one thing they can't stand is being laughed at and they're the joke of Panem," says Haymitch.

I feel dread coursing through me now, but I laugh as though Haymitch is saying something completely delightful because nothing is covering my mouth. "So, what?"

---

23 **to course through** to run through (fast and hard) – 24 **delightful** charming

"Your only defense can be you were so madly in love you weren't responsible for your actions." Haymitch pulls back and adjusts my hairband. "Got it, sweetheart?" He could be talking about anything now.

"Got it," I say. "Did you tell Peeta this?"

"Don't have to," says Haymitch. "He's already there."

"But you think I'm not?" I say, taking the opportunity to straighten a bright red bow tie Cinna must have wrestled him into.

"Since when does it matter what I think?" says Haymitch. "Better take our places." He leads me to the metal circle. "This is your night, sweetheart. Enjoy it." He kisses me on the forehead and disappears into the gloom.

I tug on my skirt, willing it to be longer, wanting it to cover the knocking in my knees. Then I realize it's pointless. My whole body's shaking like a leaf. Hopefully, it will be put down to excitement. After all, it's my night.

The damp, moldy smell beneath the stage threatens to choke me. A cold, clammy sweat breaks out on my skin and I can't rid myself of the feeling that the boards above my head are about to collapse, to bury me alive under the rubble. When I left the arena, when the trumpets played, I was supposed to be safe. From then on. For the rest of my life. But if what Haymitch says is true, and he's got no reason to lie, I've never been in such a dangerous place in my life.

It's so much worse than being hunted in the arena. There, I could only die. End of story. But out here Prim, my mother, Gale, the people of District 12, everyone I care about back home could be punished if I can't pull off the girl-driven-crazy-by-love scenario Haymitch has suggested.

---

8 bow tie [ˌboʊ.ˈtaɪ] a man's tie tied in a bow around the neck *(Fliege)*

So I still have a chance, though. Funny, in the arena, when I poured out those berries, I was only thinking of outsmarting the Gamemakers, not how my actions would reflect on the Capitol. But the Hunger Games are their weapon and you are not supposed to be able to defeat it. So now the Capitol will act as if they've been in control the whole time. As if they orchestrated the whole event, right down to the double suicide. But that will only work if I play along with them.

And Peeta … Peeta will suffer, too, if this goes wrong. But what was it Haymitch said when I asked if he had told Peeta the situation? That he had to pretend to be desperately in love?

"Don't have to. He's already there."

Already thinking ahead of me in the Games again and well aware of the danger we're in? Or … already desperately in love? I don't know. I haven't even begun to separate out my feelings about Peeta. It's too complicated. What I did as part of the Games. As opposed to what I did out of anger at the Capitol. Or because of how it would be viewed back in District 12. Or simply because it was the only decent thing to do. Or what I did because I cared about him.

These are questions to be unraveled back home, in the peace and quiet of the woods, when no one is watching. Not here with every eye upon me. But I won't have that luxury for who knows how long. And right now, the most dangerous part of the Hunger Games is about to begin.

---

20 **to be unraveled** to be explained

[Chapter 27]

The anthem booms in my ears, and then I hear Caesar Flickerman greeting the audience. Does he know how crucial it is to get every word right from now on? He must. He will want to help us. The crowd breaks into applause as the prep teams are presented. I imagine Flavius, Venia, and Octavia bouncing around and taking ridiculous, bobbing bows. It's a safe bet they're clueless. Then Effie's introduced. How long she's waited for this moment. I hope she's able to enjoy it because as misguided as Effie can be, she has a very keen instinct about certain things and must at least suspect we're in trouble. Portia and Cinna receive huge cheers, of course, they've been brilliant, had a dazzling debut. I now understand Cinna's choice of dress for me for tonight. I'll need to look as girlish and innocent as possible. Haymitch's appearance brings a round of stomping that goes on at least five minutes. Well, he's accomplished a first. Keeping not only one but two tributes alive. What if he hadn't warned me in time? Would I have acted differently? Flaunted the moment with the berries in the Capitol's face? No, I don't think so. But I could easily have been a lot less convincing than I need to be now. Right now. Because I can feel the plate lifting me up to the stage.

Blinding lights. The deafening roar rattles the metal under my feet. Then there's Peeta just a few yards away. He looks so clean and healthy and beautiful, I can hardly recognize him. But his smile is the same whether in mud or in the Capitol and when I see it, I take about three steps and fling myself into his arms. He staggers back, almost losing his balance, and that's when I realize the slim, metal

---

3 **crucial** ['kru:ʃəl] *here:* important, decisive – 9 **misguided** confused, silly – 11 **Portia and Cinna** are responsible for Katniss's appearance (clothes, make-up, etc) – 12 **dazzling** glamorous, brilliant – 17 **to flaunt** [flɑ:nt] to show shamelessly in public *(öffentlich zur Schau stellen)*

contraption in his hand is some kind of cane. He rights himself and we just cling to each other while the audience goes insane. He's kissing me and all the time I'm thinking, *Do you know? Do you know how much danger we're in?* After about ten minutes of this, Caesar Flickerman taps on his shoulder to continue the show, and Peeta just pushes him aside without even glancing at him. The audience goes berserk. Whether he knows or not, Peeta is, as usual, playing the crowd exactly right.

Finally, Haymitch interrupts us and gives us a goodnatured shove toward the victor's chair. Usually, this is a single, ornate chair from which the winning tribute watches a film of the highlights of the Games, but since there are two of us, the Gamemakers have provided a plush red velvet couch. A small one, my mother would call it a love seat, I think. I sit so close to Peeta that I'm practically on his lap, but one look from Haymitch tells me it isn't enough. Kicking off my sandals, I tuck my feet to the side and lean my head against Peeta's shoulder. His arm goes around me automatically, and I feel like I'm back in the cave, curled up against him, trying to keep warm. His shirt is made of the same yellow material as my dress, but Portia's put him in long black pants. No sandals, either, but a pair of sturdy black boots he keeps solidly planted on the stage. I wish Cinna had given me a similar outfit, I feel so vulnerable in this flimsy dress. But I guess that was the point.

Caesar Flickerman makes a few more jokes, and then it's time for the show. This will last exactly three hours and is required viewing for all of Panem. As the lights dim and the seal appears on the screen, I realize I'm unprepared for this. I do not want to watch my twenty-two fellow tributes die. I saw enough of them die the first time. My heart starts pounding and I have a strong impulse to run.

---

7 **to go berserk** *(inf)* to go mad and wild – 10 **ornate** [ɔːrˈneɪt] heavily decorated – 22 **vulnerable** weak

How have the other victors faced this alone? During the highlights, they periodically show the winner's reaction up on a box in the corner of the screen. I think back to earlier years ... some are triumphant, pumping their fists in the air, beating their chests. Most just seem stunned. All I know is that the only thing keeping me on this love seat is Peeta — his arm around my shoulder, his other hand claimed by both of mine. Of course, the previous victors didn't have the Capitol looking for a way to destroy them.

Condensing several weeks into three hours is quite a feat, especially when you consider how many cameras were going at once. Whoever puts together the highlights has to choose what sort of story to tell. This year, for the first time, they tell a love story. I know Peeta and I won, but a disproportionate amount of time is spent on us, right from the beginning. I'm glad though, because it supports the whole crazy-in-love thing that's my defense for defying the Capitol, plus it means we won't have as much time to linger over the deaths.

The first half hour or so focuses on the pre-arena events, the reaping, the chariot ride through the Capitol, our training scores, and our interviews. There's this sort of upbeat soundtrack playing under it that makes it twice as awful because, of course, almost everyone on-screen is dead.

Once we're in the arena, there's detailed coverage of the bloodbath and then the filmmakers basically alternate between shots of tributes dying and shots of us. Mostly Peeta really, there's no question he's carrying this romance thing on his shoulders. Now I see what the audience saw, how he misled the Careers about me, stayed awake the entire night under the tracker jacker tree, fought Cato to let me

---

9 **feat** achievement – 13 **disproportionate** not proportional – 15 **to defy** to show defiance *(trotzen)* – 16 **to linger** to think for a longer time about sth *(in Gedanken verweilen)* – 27 **to mislead, misled, misled** to lead in the wrong direction

escape and even while he lay in that mud bank, whispered my name in his sleep. I seem heartless in comparison — dodging fireballs, dropping nests, and blowing up supplies — until I go hunting for Rue. They play her death in full, the spearing, my failed rescue attempt, my arrow through the boy from District 1's throat, Rue drawing her last breath in my arms. And the song. I get to sing every note of the song. Something inside me shuts down and I'm too numb to feel anything. It's like watching complete strangers in another Hunger Games. But I do notice they omit the part where I covered her in flowers.

Right. Because even that smacks of rebellion.

Things pick up for me once they've announced two tributes from the same district can live and I shout out Peeta's name and then clap my hands over my mouth. If I've seemed indifferent to him earlier, I make up for it now, by finding him, nursing him back to health, going to the feast for the medicine, and being very free with my kisses. Objectively, I can see the mutts and Cato's death are as gruesome as ever, but again, I feel it happens to people I have never met.

And then comes the moment with the berries. I can hear the audience hushing one another, not wanting to miss anything. A wave of gratitude to the filmmakers sweeps over me when they end not with the announcement of our victory, but with me pounding on the glass door of the hovercraft, screaming Peeta's name as they try to revive him.

In terms of survival, it's my best moment all night.

The anthem's playing yet again and we rise as President Snow himself takes the stage followed by a little girl carrying a cushion that holds the crown. There's just one crown, though, and you can

---

9 **to omit** to leave out – 11 **to smack of** to seem like

hear the crowd's confusion — whose head will he place it on? — until President Snow gives it a twist and it separates into two halves. He places the first around Peeta's brow with a smile. He's still smiling when he settles the second on my head, but his eyes, just inches from mine, are as unforgiving as a snake's.

That's when I know that even though both of us would have eaten the berries, I am to blame for having the idea. I'm the instigator. I'm the one to be punished.

7 **instigator** initiator

Extract 3: President Snow (from the second novel, *Catching Fire*)

[Katniss has returned home to District 12 where she now lives with her family in the Victors Village.]

In my mind, President Snow should be viewed in front of marble pillars hung with oversized flags. It's jarring to see him surrounded by the ordinary objects in the room. Like taking the lid off a pot and finding a fanged viper instead of stew.

What could he be doing here? My mind rushes back to the opening days of other Victory Tours. I remember seeing the winning tributes with their mentors and stylists. Even some high government officials have made appearances occasionally. But I have never seen President Snow. He attends celebrations in the Capitol. Period.

If he's made the journey all the way from his city, it can only mean one thing. I'm in serious trouble. And if I am, so is my family. A shiver goes through me when I think of the proximity of my mother and sister to this man who despises me. Will always despise me. Because I outsmarted his sadistic Hunger Games, made the Capitol look foolish, and consequently undermined his control.

All I was doing was trying to keep Peeta and myself alive. Any act of rebellion was purely coincidental. But when the Capitol decrees that only one tribute can live and you have the audacity to challenge it, I guess that's a rebellion in itself. My only defense was pretending that I was driven insane by a passionate love for Peeta. So we were both allowed to live. To be crowned victors. To go home and

---

5 **marble** made of marble *(aus Marmor)* – 6 **jarring** unfitting *(unpassend)* – 8 **fanged** with fangs, i.e long sharp teeth – 13 **Period.** *(AE, coll)* And that's it. *(Schluss. / Punkt.)* – 16 **proximity** [-'---] closeness – 21 **coincidental** happening by chance, not intended – 22 **audacity** [-'---] *Frechheit* – 22 **to challenge** *herausfordern, trotzen* – 24 **insane** [-'-] mad

celebrate and wave good-bye to the cameras and be left alone. Until now.

Perhaps it is the newness of the house or the shock of seeing him or the mutual understanding that he could have me killed in a second that makes me feel like the intruder. As if this is his home and I'm the uninvited party. So I don't welcome him or offer him a chair. I don't say anything. In fact, I treat him as if he's a real snake, the venomous kind. I stand motionless, my eyes locked on him, considering plans of retreat.

"I think we'll make this whole situation a lot simpler by agreeing not to lie to each other," he says. "What do you think?"

I think my tongue has frozen and speech will be impossible, so I surprise myself by answering back in a steady voice, "Yes, I think that would save time."

President Snow smiles and I notice his lips for the first time. I'm expecting snake lips, which is to say none. But his are overly full, the skin stretched too tight. I have to wonder if his mouth has been altered to make him more appealing. If so, it was a waste of time and money, because he's not appealing at all. "My advisors were concerned you would be difficult, but you're not planning on being difficult, are you?" he asks.

"No," I answer.

"That's what I told them. I said any girl who goes to such lengths to preserve her life isn't going to be interested in throwing it away with both hands. And then there's her family to think of. Her mother, her sister, and all those … cousins." By the way he lingers on the word "cousins," I can tell he knows that Gale and I don't share a family tree.

---

4 **mutual** *gegenseitig* – 5 **intruder** sb entering a place without a right to do so – 8 **venomous** poisonous – 18 **to alter** to change – 18 **appealing** attractive, likable – 20 **concerned** worried – 23 **to go to (great) lengths** to do whatever is necessary to achieve sth – 26 **to linger on** *here:* to pause

Well, it's all on the table now. Maybe that's better. I don't do well with ambiguous threats. I'd much rather know the score.

"Let's sit." President Snow takes a seat at the large desk of polished wood where Prim does her homework and my mother her budgets. Like our home, this is a place that he has no right, but ultimately every right, to occupy. I sit in front of the desk on one of the carved, straight-backed chairs. It's made for someone taller than I am, so only my toes rest on the ground.

"I have a problem, Miss Everdeen," says President Snow. "A problem that began the moment you pulled out those poisonous berries in the arena.

"That was the moment when I guessed that if the Gamemakers had to choose between watching Peeta and me commit suicide—which would mean having no victor—and letting us both live, they would take the latter.

"If the Head Gamemaker, Seneca Crane, had had any brains, he'd have blown you to dust right then. But he had an unfortunate sentimental streak. So here you are. Can you guess where he is?" he asks.

I nod because, by the way he says it, it's clear that Seneca Crane has been executed. The smell of roses and blood has grown stronger now that only a desk separates us. There's a rose in President Snow's lapel, which at least suggests a source of the flower perfume, but it must be genetically enhanced, because no real rose reeks like that. As for the blood … I don't know.

"After that, there was nothing to do but let you play out your little scenario. And you were pretty good, too, with the love-crazed schoolgirl bit. The people in the Capitol were quite convinced.

---

2 **ambiguous** not clearly defined – 2 **to know the score** to know what's what *(wissen, woran man ist)* – 5 **ultimately** in the end *(letztlich)* – 6 **carved** cut in decorative patterns *(geschnitzt)* – 12 **Gamemaker** a person who "designs" the annual Hunger Game entertainment – 18 **streak** tendency, quality in one's character – 23 **lapel** [lə'pel] the part of the front of a coat or jacket that is folded back – 28 **convinced** *überzeugt*

Unfortunately, not everyone in the districts fell for your act," he says.

My face must register at least a flicker of bewilderment, because he addresses it.

"This, of course, you don't know. You have no access to information about the mood in other districts. In several of them, however, people viewed your little trick with the berries as an act of defiance, not an act of love. And if a girl from District Twelve of all places can defy the Capitol and walk away unharmed, what is to stop them from doing the same?" he says. "What is to prevent, say, an uprising?"

It takes a moment for his last sentence to sink in. Then the full weight of it hits me. "There have been uprisings?" I ask, both chilled and somewhat elated by the possibility.

"Not yet. But they'll follow if the course of things doesn't change. And uprisings have been known to lead to revolution." President Snow rubs a spot over his left eyebrow, the very spot where I myself get headaches. "Do you have any idea what that would mean? How many people would die? What conditions those left would have to face? Whatever problems anyone may have with the Capitol, believe me when I say that if it released its grip on the districts for even a short time, the entire system would collapse."

I'm taken aback by the directness and even the sincerity of this speech. As if his primary concern is the welfare of the citizens of Panem, when nothing could be further from the truth. I don't know how I dare to say the next words, but I do. "It must be very fragile, if a handful of berries can bring it down."

---

1 **to fall for sth** to be fooled by sth – 3 **bewilderment** [bɪˈwɪldɚmənt] confusion – 5 **access** [ˈækses] means (way) of getting sth – 8 **defiance** [dɪˈfaɪəns] opposition, challenge – 11 **uprising** revolt – 14 **elated** joyful, extremely happy – 21 **to release** to let go – 23 **to be taken aback** to be surprised – 26 **fragile** [ˈfrædʒəl] easily broken or destroyed

There's a long pause while he examines me. Then he simply says, "It is fragile, but not in the way that you suppose."

There's a knock at the door, and the Capitol man sticks his head in. "Her mother wants to know if you want tea."

"I would. I would like tea," says the president. The door opens wider, and there stands my mother, holding a tray with a china tea set she brought to the Seam when she married. "Set it here, please." He places his book on the corner of the desk and pats the center.

My mother sets the tray on the desk. It holds a china teapot and cups, cream and sugar, and a plate of cookies. They are beautifully iced with softly colored flowers. The frosting work can only be Peeta's.

"What a welcome sight. You know, it's funny how often people forget that presidents need to eat, too," President Snow says charmingly. Well, it seems to relax my mother a bit, anyway.

"Can I get you anything else? I can cook something more substantial if you're hungry," she offers.

"No, this could not be more perfect. Thank you," he says, clearly dismissing her. My mother nods, shoots me a glance, and goes. President Snow pours tea for both of us and fills his with cream and sugar, then takes a long time stirring. I sense he has had his say and is waiting for me to respond.

"I didn't mean to start any uprisings," I tell him.

"I believe you. It doesn't matter. Your stylist turned out to be prophetic in his wardrobe choice. Katniss Everdeen, the girl who was on fire, you have provided a spark that, left unattended, may grow to an inferno that destroys Panem," he says.

"Why don't you just kill me now?" I blurt out.

---

11 **iced** covered with frosting *(= Zuckerguss)* – 16 **something more substantial** *etwas Habhafteres* – 19 **to dismiss sb** to tell sb to go away – 19 **glance** a quick look – 21 **to stir** *rühren* – 21 **to sense** to feel – 25 **wardrobe** *here:* clothing – 26 **spark** small, burning piece of sth that is thrown off from a fire *(Funke)* – 26 **unattended** not taken care of

"Publicly?" he asks. "That would only add fuel to the flames."

"Arrange an accident, then," I say.

"Who would buy it?" he asks. "Not you, if you were watching."

"Then just tell me what you want me to do. I'll do it," I say.

"If only it were that simple." He picks up one of the flowered cookies and examines it. "Lovely. Your mother made these?"

"Peeta." And for the first time, I find I can't hold his gaze. I reach for my tea but set it back down when I hear the cup rattling against the saucer. To cover I quickly take a cookie.

"Peeta. How *is* the love of your life?" he asks.

"Good," I say.

"At what point did he realize the exact degree of your indifference?" he asks, dipping his cookie in his tea.

"I'm not indifferent," I say.

"But perhaps not as taken with the young man as you would have the country believe," he says.

"Who says I'm not?" I say.

"I do," says the president. "And I wouldn't be here if I were the only person who had doubts. How's the handsome cousin?"

"I don't know … I don't …" My revulsion at this conversation, at discussing my feelings for two of the people I care most about with President Snow, chokes me off.

"Speak, Miss Everdeen. Him I can easily kill off if we don't come to a happy resolution," he says. "You aren't doing him a favor by disappearing into the woods with him each Sunday."

If he knows this, what else does he know? And how does he know it? Many people could tell him that Gale and I spend our Sundays hunting. Don't we show up at the end of each one loaded down with

---

3 **to buy sth** *(coll)* to believe sth – 9 **to cover** *here:* in order to hide this – 12 **indifference** lack of interest or, here, love *(Gleichgültigkeit)* – 15 **to be taken with sb** to be in love with sb – 20 **revulsion** strong feeling of dislike – 22 **it chokes me off** it makes it impossible for me to speak

game? Haven't we for years? The real question is what he thinks goes on in the woods beyond District 12. Surely they haven't been tracking us in there. Or have they? Could we have been followed? That seems impossible. At least by a person. Cameras? That never crossed my mind until this moment. The woods have always been our place of safety, our place beyond the reach of the Capitol, where we're free to say what we feel, be who we are. At least before the Games. If we've been watched since, what have they seen? Two people hunting, saying treasonous things against the Capitol, yes. But not two people in love, which seems to be President Snow's implication. We are safe on that charge. Unless … unless …

It only happened once. It was fast and unexpected, but it did happen.

After Peeta and I got home from the Games, it was several weeks before I saw Gale alone. First there were the obligatory celebrations. A banquet for the victors that only the most high-ranking people were invited to. A holiday for the whole district with free food and entertainers brought in from the Capitol. Parcel Day, the first of twelve, in which food packages were delivered to every person in the district. That was my favorite. To see all those hungry kids in the Seam running around, waving cans of applesauce, tins of meat, even candy. Back home, too big to carry, would be bags of grain, cans of oil. To know that once a month for a year they would all receive another parcel. That was one of the few times I actually felt good about winning the Games.

So between the ceremonies and events and the reporters documenting my every move as I presided and thanked and kissed Peeta for the audience, I had no privacy at all. After a few weeks, things finally died down. The camera crews and reporters packed

3 **to track** to follow or watch the path of sb or sth e.g. by using electronic devices – 9 **treasonous** *verräterisch* – 11 **implication** sth which is suggested but not directly mentioned

up and went home. Peeta and I assumed the cool relationship we've had ever since. My family settled into our house in the Victor's Village. The everyday life of District 12—workers to the mines, kids to school—resumed its usual pace. I waited until I thought the coast was really clear, and then one Sunday, without telling anyone, I got up hours before dawn and took off for the woods.

The weather was still warm enough that I didn't need a jacket. I packed along a bag filled with special foods, cold chicken and cheese and bakery bread and oranges. Down at my old house, I put on my hunting boots. As usual, the fence was not charged and it was simple to slip into the woods and retrieve my bow and arrows. I went to our place, Gale's and mine, where we had shared breakfast the morning of the reaping that sent me into the Games.

I waited at least two hours. I'd begun to think that he'd given up on me in the weeks that had passed. Or that he no longer cared about me. Hated me even. And the idea of losing him forever, my best friend, the only person I'd ever trusted with my secrets, was so painful I couldn't stand it. Not on top of everything else that had happened. I could feel my eyes tearing up and my throat starting to close the way it does when I get upset.

Then I looked up and there he was, ten feet away, just watching me. Without even thinking, I jumped up and threw my arms around him, making some weird sound that combined laughing, choking, and crying. He was holding me so tightly that I couldn't see his face, but it was a really long time before he let me go and then he didn't have much choice, because I'd gotten this unbelievably loud case of the hiccups and had to get a drink.

We did what we always did that day. Ate breakfast. Hunted and fished and gathered. Talked about people in town. But not about us,

4 **the coast is clear** there is no danger – 11 **to retrieve sth** to find and get sth – 19 **tearing up** filling with tears – 27 **hiccup** *Schluckauf* – 29 **to gather** to collect berries and herbs

his new life in the mines, my time in the arena. Just about other things. By the time we were at the hole in the fence that's nearest the Hob, I think I really believed that things could be the same. That we could go on as we always had. I'd given all the game to Gale to trade since we had so much food now. I told him I'd skip the Hob, even though I was looking forward to going there, because my mother and sister didn't even know I'd gone hunting and they'd be wondering where I was. Then suddenly, as I was suggesting I take over the daily snare run, he took my face in his hands and kissed me.

I was completely unprepared. You would think that after all the hours I'd spent with Gale—watching him talk and laugh and frown—that I would know all there was to know about his lips. But I hadn't imagined how warm they would feel pressed against my own. Or how those hands, which could set the most intricate of snares, could as easily entrap me. I think I made some sort of noise in the back of my throat, and I vaguely remember my fingers, curled tightly closed, resting on his chest. Then he let go and said, "I had to do that. At least once." And he was gone.

Despite the fact that the sun was setting and my family would be worried, I sat by a tree next to the fence. I tried to decide how I felt about the kiss, if I had liked it or resented it, but all I really remembered was the pressure of Gale's lips and the scent of the oranges that still lingered on his skin. It was pointless comparing it with the many kisses I'd exchanged with Peeta. I still hadn't figured out if any of those counted. Finally I went home.

That week I managed the snares and dropped off the meat with Hazelle. But I didn't see Gale until Sunday. I had this whole speech worked out, about how I didn't want a boyfriend and never planned

---

5 **to skip** to leave out, to not go to anymore – 15 **intricate** complicated – 22 **to resent sth** [rɪ'zent] to be slightly angry about (and/or not like) sth – 25 **to figure out** ['fɪgjʊˌraʊt] to find out, to work out

on marrying, but I didn't end up using it. Gale acted as if the kiss had never happened. Maybe he was waiting for me to say something. Or kiss him back. Instead I just pretended it had never happened, either. But it had. Gale had shattered some invisible barrier between us and, with it, any hope I had of resuming our old, uncomplicated friendship. Whatever I pretended, I could never look at his lips in quite the same way.

This all flashes through my head in an instant as President Snow's eyes bore into me on the heels of his threat to kill Gale. How stupid I've been to think the Capitol would just ignore me once I'd returned home! Maybe I didn't know about the potential uprisings. But I know they were angry with me. Instead of acting with the extreme caution the situation called for, what have I done? From the president's point of view, I've ignored Peeta and flaunted my preference for Gale's company before the whole district. And by doing so made it clear I was, in fact, mocking the Capitol. Now I've endangered Gale and his family and my family and Peeta, too, by my carelessness.

"Please don't hurt Gale," I whisper. "He's just my friend. He's been my friend for years. That's all that's between us. Besides, everyone thinks we're cousins now."

"I'm only interested in how it affects your dynamic with Peeta, thereby affecting the mood in the districts," he says.

"It will be the same on the tour. I'll be in love with him just as I was," I say.

"Just as you are," corrects President Snow.

"Just as I am," I confirm.

"Only you'll have to do even better if the uprisings are to be averted," he says. "This tour will be your only chance to turn things around."

---

9 on the heels of immediately after – 13 **to call for sth** to demand sth *(erfordern)* – 14 **to flaunt** to show off, to make sure everyone notices – 27 **to confirm** *bestätigen* – 29 **to avert** to prevent *(abwenden)*

“I know. I will. I’ll convince everyone in the districts that I wasn’t defying the Capitol, that I was crazy with love,” I say.

President Snow rises and dabs his puffy lips with a napkin. “Aim higher in case you fall short.”

“What do you mean? How can I aim higher?” I ask.

“Convince *me*,” he says. He drops the napkin and retrieves his book. I don’t watch him as he heads for the door, so I flinch when he whispers in my ear. “By the way, I know about the kiss.” Then the door clicks shut behind him.

(6,612 words)

4 **to fall short** to fail – 7 **to flinch** to move away suddenly when surprised by sth

Make notes here on what this section has contributed to your bigger picture of "Visions of the Future".

3 Medical ethics

Introduction

This section specifically looks at the technological and scientific developments in the medical field and the ethics encircling them. Due to such discoveries and advancements proceeding at such a high rate, regulations struggle to keep up with potential moral consequences.

The first text deals particularly with technology in the field of genetics and the sequencing of genes, where possible ethical issues are brought to the forefront.

The second text focuses primarily on the ethical issues raised by stem cells, which in the past could only be harvested from embryos, and offers a solution to this problem that could have an immense impact on medicine and medical research.

There is, of course, a dark side to medical ethics but no, they do not have cookies – they have body parts. Because the demand for body parts is so high and organ donors in low supply, a "gray" market has been created to fulfill those needs. The last article in this section investigates a company that makes a profit from selling body parts privately. The journalist reveals how they manage to skirt around laws and regulations in order to do so.

Tasks

Pre-reading tasks

Think: Imagine there is a new cure for acne in which you only need one shot and you will have perfect skin forever. Would you take the shot? What if this medicine can only be made by harming someone or something else? Would you still take it?

Watch: Before reading the articles, watch this **video about CRISPR** and take notes.
Then: describe and assess what CRISPR is.

The materials that you need can be accessed via online link fpcyxaw or using the Klett Augmented app (scan page 161).

Text 1: Article
Designer babies: an ethical horror waiting to happen?

Philip Ball, The Observer, January 2017

Nearly 40 years since the first 'test-tube baby', how close are we to editing out all of our genetic imperfections – and should we even try to do so?

Comfortably seated in the fertility clinic with Vivaldi playing softly in the background, you and your partner are brought coffee and a folder. Inside the folder is an embryo menu. Each embryo has a description, something like this:

Embryo 78 – male

- No serious early onset diseases, but a carrier for phenylketonuria (a metabolic malfunction that can cause behavioural and mental disorders. Carriers just have one copy of the gene, so don't get the condition themselves).
- Higher than average risk of type 2 diabetes and colon cancer.
- Lower than average risk of asthma and autism.
- Dark eyes, light brown hair, male pattern baldness.
- 40 % chance of coming in the top half in SAT tests.

---

10 **early onset disease** a disease which sb will get early in life – 11 **metabolic** [ˌmet̬əˈbɑːlɪk] *metabolisch, Stoffwechsel-* – 11 **malfunction** failure to work normally – 14 **colon cancer** *Dickdarmkrebs* – 16 **male pattern baldness** losing hair in the way that men generally do (e.g. hair falls out in middle age) – 17 **SAT** (*abb* for: **Scholastic Assessment Test**) academic test used mainly in the US to assess students' readiness for university

There are 200 of these embryos to choose from, all made by in vitro fertilisation (IVF) from you and your partner's eggs and sperm. So, over to you. Which will you choose?

If there's any kind of future for "designer babies", it might look something like this. It's a long way from the image conjured up when artificial conception, and perhaps even artificial gestation, were first mooted as a serious scientific possibility. Inspired by predictions about the future of reproductive technology by the biologists JBS Haldane and Julian Huxley in the 1920s, Huxley's brother Aldous wrote a satirical novel about it.

That book was, of course, *Brave New World*, published in 1932. Set in the year 2540, it describes a society whose population is grown in vats in an impersonal central hatchery, graded into five tiers of different intelligence by chemical treatment of the embryos. There are no parents as such – families are considered obscene. Instead, the gestating fetuses and babies are tended by workers in white overalls, "their hands gloved with a pale, corpse-coloured rubber", under white, dead lights.

Brave New World has become the inevitable reference point for all media discussion of new advances in reproductive technology. Whether it's *Newsweek* reporting in 1978 on 🔗 **the birth of Louise Brown**, the first "test-tube baby" (the inaccurate phrase speaks volumes) as a "cry round the brave new world", or the *New York Times* announcing "The brave new world of three-parent IVF" in 2014, the message is that we are heading towards Huxley's hatchery with its racks of tailor-made babies in their "numbered test tubes".

---

1 **in vitro fertilisation** *künstliche Befruchtung* – 6 **gestation** [dʒes'teɪʃən] period of time that the embryo/fetus develops before birth or, here, before it can survive in the world, with parents' help – 7 **mooted** suggested for discussion – 13 **vat** large container that hold liquids – 13 **hatchery** ['hætʃəri] *Brutplatz* – 15 **obscene** [ɑ:b'si:n] offensive, disgusting – 17 **corpse-coloured** the same colour as a dead body – 21 🔗 **For online link, use code fpcyxaw at klett-sprachen.de. For Klett Augmented, scan page 161.** – 22 **speaks volumes** *(idm)* is very revealing *(spricht Bände)*

The spectre of a harsh, impersonal and authoritarian dystopia always looms in these discussions of reproductive control and selection. Novelist Kazuo Ishiguro, whose 2005 novel, 🔗 <u>**Never Let Me Go**</u>, described children produced and reared as organ donors, last month warned that thanks to advances in gene editing, “we’re coming close to the point where we can, objectively in some sense, create people who are superior to others”.

But the prospect of genetic portraits of IVF embryos paints a rather different picture. If it happens at all, the aim will be not to engineer societies but to attract consumers. Should we allow that? Even if we do, would a list of dozens or even hundreds of embryos with diverse yet sketchy genetic endowments be of any use to anyone?

The shadow of *Frankenstein*’s monster haunted the fraught discussion of IVF in the 1970s and 80s, and the misleading term “three-parent baby” to refer to embryos made by the technique of mitochondrial transfer – moving healthy versions of the energy-generating cell compartments called mitochondria from a donor cell to an egg with faulty, potentially fatal versions – insinuates that there must be something “unnatural” about the procedure.

Every new advance puts a fresh spark of life into Huxley’s monstrous vision. Ishiguro’s dire forecast was spurred by the gene-editing method called Crispr-Cas9, developed in 2012, which uses natural enzymes to target and snip genes with pinpoint accuracy. Thanks to Crispr-Cas9, it seems likely that gene therapies – eliminating mutant genes that cause some severe, mostly very rare

---

1 **spectre** ['spektə˞] ghost, highly feared event – 3 🔗 **For online link, use code fpcyxaw at klett-sprachen.de. For Klett Augmented, scan page 161.** – 5 **gene editing** ['ʤi:n.ˌedɪtɪŋ] changing the pattern and contents of genes *(Genbearbeitung)* – 12 **sketchy** incomplete, fragmented – 12 **endowment** gift, characteristic – 14 **fraught** [frɑ:t] worried, anxious – 19 **insinuate** [ɪn'sɪnjueɪt] imply or suggest in an unpleasant way – 22 **dire** [daɪə˞] pessimistic – 24 **enzyme** ['enzaɪm] *Enzym* – 24 **to snip** *(inf)* to cut

diseases – might finally bear fruit, if they can be shown to be safe for human use. Clinical trials are now under way.

But modified babies? Crispr-Cas9 has already been used to genetically modify (nonviable) human embryos in China, to see if it is possible in principle – the results were mixed. And Kathy Niakan of the Francis Crick Institute in the UK has been granted a licence by the Human Fertilisation and Embryology Authority (HFEA) to use Crispr-Cas9 on embryos a few days old to find out more about problems in these early stages of development that can lead to miscarriage and other reproductive problems.

Most countries have not yet legislated on genetic modification in human reproduction, but of those that have, all have banned it. The idea of using Crispr-Cas9 for human reproduction is largely rejected in principle by the medical research community. A team of scientists warned in *Nature* less than two years ago that genetic manipulation of the germ line (sperm and egg cells) by methods like Crispr-Cas9, even if focused initially on improving health, "could start us down 🔗 **a path towards non-therapeutic genetic enhancement**".

Besides, there seems to be little need for gene editing in reproduction. It would be a difficult, expensive and uncertain way to achieve what can mostly be achieved already in other ways, particularly by just selecting an embryo that has or lacks the gene in question. "Almost everything you can accomplish by gene editing, you can accomplish by embryo selection," says bioethicist Henry Greely of Stanford University in California.

---

1 **bear fruit** produce results – 4 **nonviable** unable to survive – 10 **miscarriage** *Fehlgeburt* – 11 **legislate** pass laws – 18 🔗 **For online link, use code fpcyxaw at klett-sprachen.de. For Klett Augmented, scan page 161.** – 19 **enhancement** improvement – 23 **to lack** to be without sth, in need of sth – 24 **to accomplish** achieve or complete sth successfully – 25 **bioethicist** [baɪoʊ'eθɪsɪst] scientist focused on moral questions raised by new situations or technology

Because of unknown health risks and widespread public distrust of gene editing, bioethicist Ronald Green of Dartmouth College in New Hampshire says he does not foresee widespread use of Crispr-Cas9 in the next two decades, even for the prevention of genetic disease, let alone for designer babies. However, Green does see gene editing appearing on the menu eventually, and perhaps not just for medical therapies. "It is unavoidably in our future," he says, "and I believe that it will become one of the central foci of our social debates later in this century and in the century beyond." He warns that this might be accompanied by "serious errors and health problems as unknown genetic side effects in 'edited' children and populations begin to manifest themselves".

For now, though, if there's going to be anything even vaguely resembling the popular designer-baby fantasy, Greely says it will come from embryo selection, not genetic manipulation. Embryos produced by IVF will be genetically screened – parts or all of their DNA will be read to deduce which gene variants they carry – and the prospective parents will be able to choose which embryos to implant in the hope of achieving a pregnancy. Greely foresees that new methods of harvesting or producing human eggs, along with advances in preimplantation genetic diagnosis (PGD) of IVF embryos, will make selection much more viable and appealing, and thus more common, in 20 years' time.

PGD is already used by couples who know that they carry genes for specific inherited diseases so that they can identify embryos that do not have those genes. The testing, generally on three- to five-day-old embryos, is conducted in around 5 % of IVF cycles in the US. In the UK it is performed under licence from the HFEA, which

---

4 **decade** ten years – 12 **to manifest** show, demonstrate – 16 **to screen** test, observe, examine – 17 **to deduce** [dɪ'du:s] to find out by a process of elimination – 21 **preimplantation genetic diagnosis** *Präimplantationsdiagnostik*

permits screening for around 250 diseases including thalassemia, early-onset Alzheimer's and cystic fibrosis.

As a way of "designing" your baby, PGD is currently unattractive. "Egg harvesting is unpleasant and risky and doesn't give you that many eggs," says Greely, and the success rate for implanted embryos is still typically about one in three. But that will change, he says, thanks to developments that will make human eggs much more abundant and conveniently available, coupled to the possibility of screening their genomes quickly and cheaply.

Advances in methods for reading the genetic code recorded in our chromosomes are going to make it a routine possibility for every one of us – certainly, every newborn child – to have our genes sequenced. "In the next 10 years or so, the chances are that many people in rich countries will have large chunks of their genetic information in their electronic medical records," says Greely.

But using genetic data to predict what kind of person an embryo would become is far more complicated than is often implied. Seeking to justify unquestionably important research on the genetic basis of human health, researchers haven't done much to dispel simplistic ideas about how genes make us. Talk of "IQ genes", "gay genes" and "musical genes" has led to a widespread perception that there is a straightforward one-to-one relationship between our genes and our traits. In general, it's anything but.

There are thousands of mostly rare and nasty genetic diseases that can be pinpointed to a specific gene mutation. Most more common diseases or medical predispositions – for example, diabetes, heart disease or certain types of cancer – are linked to several or

---

1 **screening** testing – 1 **thalassemia** blood disorder passed down in genes – 2 **cystic fibrosis** ['sɪstɪk.faɪ'broʊsɪs] *Mukoviszidose* – 8 **abundant** plentiful, more than enough – 13 **sequenced** put in correct order – 18 **to justify** prove sth is right or OK to do *(rechtfertigen)* – 19 **dispel** dismiss, eliminate – 23 **anything but** *(adv)* the exact opposite – 26 **predisposition** tendency or vulnerability to certain conditions

even many genes, can't be predicted with any certainty, and depend also on environmental factors such as diet.

When it comes to more complex things like personality and intelligence, we know very little. Even if they are strongly inheritable – it's estimated that up to 80 % of intelligence, as measured by IQ, is inherited – we don't know much at all about which genes are involved, and not for want of looking.

At best, Greely says, PGD might tell a prospective parent things like "there's a 60 % chance of this child getting in the top half at school, or a 13 % chance of being in the top 10 %". That's not much use.

We might do better for "cosmetic" traits such as hair or eye colour. Even these "turn out to be more complicated than a lot of people thought," Greely says, but as the number of people whose genomes have been sequenced increases, the predictive ability will improve substantially.

Ewan Birney, director of the European Bioinformatics Institute near Cambridge, points out that, even if other countries don't choose to constrain and regulate PGD in the way the HFEA does in the UK, it will be very far from a crystal ball.

Nearly anything you can measure for humans, he says, can be studied through genetics, and analysing the statistics for huge numbers of people often reveals some genetic component. But that information "is not very predictive on an individual basis," says Birney. "I've had my genome sequenced on the cheap, and it doesn't tell me very much. We've got to get away from the idea that your DNA is your destiny."

---

5 **IQ** *abr* intelligence quotient, test to measure intellect – 7 **not for want of looking** i.e. we looked hard, but couldn't find anything – 19 **constrain** restrict, limit – 20 **it will be very far from a crystal ball** i.e. it will be easy to predict (to look into the **crystal ball** = *in die Glaskugel schauen*) – 25 **on the cheap** for very little money

If the genetic basis of attributes like intelligence and musicality is too thinly spread and unclear to make selection practical, then tweaking by genetic manipulation certainly seems off the menu too. “I don’t think we are going to see superman or a split in the species any time soon,” says Greely, “because we just don’t know enough and are unlikely to for a long time – or maybe for ever.”

If this is all “designer babies” could mean even in principle – freedom from some specific but rare diseases, knowledge of rather trivial aspects of appearance, but only vague, probabilistic information about more general traits like health, attractiveness and intelligence – will people go for it in large enough numbers to sustain an industry?

Greely suspects, even if it is used at first only to avoid serious genetic diseases, that we need to start thinking hard about the options we might be faced with. “Choices will be made,” he says, “and if informed people do not participate in making those choices, ignorant people will make them.”

Green thinks that technological advances could make “design” increasingly versatile. In the next 40–50 years, he says, “we’ll start seeing the use of gene editing and reproductive technologies for enhancement: blond hair and blue eyes, improved athletic abilities, enhanced reading skills or numeracy, and so on.”

He’s less optimistic about the consequences, saying that we will then see social tensions “as the well-to-do exploit technologies that make them even better off”, increasing the relatively worsened health status of the world’s poor. As Greely points out, a perfectly feasible 10–20 % improvement in health via PGD, added to the comparable advantage that wealth already brings, could lead to a

---

3 **tweaking** making small changes – 4 **a split in the species** i.e. making a group of people that are biologically and genetically different from the “old” group – 19 **versatile** ['vɚrsət̬ᵊl] adaptable, adjustable – 22 **numeracy** ability with numbers – 24 **the well-to-do** *(pl)* rich people – 24 **to exploit** take advantage or make use of sth unfairly – 27 **feasible** reasonable, achievable

widening of the health gap between rich and poor, both within a society and between nations.

Others doubt that there will be any great demand for embryo selection, especially if genetic forecasts remain sketchy about the most desirable traits. "Where there is a serious problem, such as a deadly condition, or an existing obstacle, such as infertility, I would not be surprised to see people take advantage of technologies such as embryo selection," says law professor and bioethicist R Alta Charo of the University of Wisconsin. "But we already have evidence that people do not flock to technologies when they can conceive without assistance."

The poor take-up of sperm banks offering "superior" sperm, she says, already shows that. For most women, "the emotional significance of reproduction outweighs any notion of 'optimisation'". Charo feels that "our ability to love one another with all our imperfections and foibles outweighs any notion of 'improving' our children through genetics".

All the same, societies are going to face tough choices about how to regulate an industry that offers PGD with an ever-widening scope. "Technologies are very amoral," says Birney. "Societies have to decide how to use them" – and different societies will make different choices.

One of the easiest things to screen for is sex. Gender-specific abortion is formally forbidden in most countries, although it still happens in places such as China and India where there has been a strong cultural preference for boys. But prohibiting selection by gender is another matter. How could it even be implemented and policed? By creating some kind of quota system?

---

6 **infertility** *Unfruchtbarkeit* – 12 **take-up** *here:* acceptance – 14 **optimisation** effectively used – 16 **foibles** ['fɔɪbᵊlz] small weaknesses or flaws – 16 **to outweigh any notion (of)** *here*: be more important than all other thoughts (about) – 18 **tough** [tʌf] difficult

And what would selection against genetic disabilities do to those people who have them? “They have a lot to be worried about here,” says Greely. “In terms of whether society thinks I should have been born, but also in terms of how much medical research there is into diseases, how well understood it is for practitioners and how much social support there is.”

Once selection beyond avoidance of genetic disease becomes an option – and it does seem likely – the ethical and legal aspects are a minefield. When is it proper for governments to coerce people into, or prohibit them from, particular choices, such as not selecting for a disability? How can one balance individual freedoms and social consequences?

“The most important consideration for me,” says Charo, “is to be clear about the distinct roles of personal morality, by which individuals decide whether to seek out technological assistance, versus the role of government, which can prohibit, regulate or promote technology.”

She adds: “Too often we discuss these technologies as if personal morality or particular religious views are a sufficient basis for governmental action. But one must ground government action in a stronger set of concerns about promoting the wellbeing of all individuals while permitting the widest range of personal liberty of conscience and choice.”

“For better or worse, human beings will not forgo the opportunity to take their evolution into their own hands,” says Green. “Will that make our lives happier and better? I’m far from sure.”

---

7 **avoidance** *Vermeidung* – 9 **to coerce** [koʊ'ɜrs] **sb into doing sth** force an unwilling person to do sth – 16 **to prohibit** prevent, outlaw – 16 **to regulate** impose set of rules or laws – 17 **to promote** encourage, aid – 21 **set of concerns** series of issues – 22 **liberty of conscience and choice** freedom to follow personal morals and make choices – 24 **to forgo** go without *(verzichten (auf))*

Easy pickings: the future of designer babies

The simplest and surest way to "design" a baby is not to construct its genome by pick'n'mix gene editing but to produce a huge number of embryos and read their genomes to find the one that most closely matches your desires.

Two technological advances are needed for this to happen, says bioethicist Henry Greely of Stanford University in California. The production of embryos for IVF must become easier, more abundant and less unpleasant. And gene sequencing must be fast and cheap enough to reveal the traits an embryo will have. Put them together and you have "Easy PGD" (preimplantation genetic diagnosis): a cheap and painless way of generating large numbers of human embryos and then screening their entire genomes for desired characteristics.

"To get much broader use of PGD, you need a better way to get eggs," Greely says. "The more eggs you can get, the more attractive PGD becomes." One possibility is a one-off medical intervention that extracts a slice of a woman's ovary and freezes it for future ripening and harvesting of eggs. It sounds drastic, but would not be much worse than current egg-extraction and embryo-implantation methods. And it could give access to thousands of eggs for future use.

An even more dramatic approach would be to grow eggs from stem cells – the cells from which all other tissue types can be derived. Some stem cells are present in umbilical blood, which could be harvested at a person's birth and frozen for later use to grow organs – or eggs.

Even mature cells that have advanced beyond the stem-cell stage and become specific tissue types can be returned to a stem-cell-like

3 **pick'n'mix** *(inf)* selected – 17 **one-off** *(adj)* unique (it only happens once) *(einmalig)* – 18 **ovary** *Eierstock* – 24 **derive** make, procure – 25 **umbilical blood** [ʌm'bɪlɪkᵊl.blʌd] blood from the umbilical cord *(Nabelschnur)*

state by treating them with biological molecules called growth factors. Last October, a team in Japan reported that they had made mouse eggs this way from skin cells, and fertilised them to create apparently healthy and fertile mouse pups.

Thanks to technological advances, the cost of human whole-genome sequencing has plummeted. In 2009 it cost around $50,000; today it is more like $1,500, which is why several private companies can now offer this service. In a few decades it could cost just a few dollars per genome. Then it becomes feasible to think of PGD for hundreds of embryos at a time.

"The science for safe and effective Easy PGD is likely to exist some time in the next 20 to 10 years," says Greely. He thinks it will then become common for children to be conceived through IVF using selected genomes. He forecasts that this will lead to "the coming obsolescence of sex" for procreation.

(2,985 words)

---

3 to fertilise *befruchten* – **4 pup** baby (dog or mouse) – **6 to plummet** fall or decrease drastically – **15 obsolescence** [ˌɑːbsəˈlesᵊnts] process of sth becoming outdated

Text 2: Article
Look, no embryos! The future of ethical stem cells

Alok Jha, The Observer, March 2011

For years, ethical issues hampered progress in stem cell research. Now, experts believe that developments in reprogrammed 'iPS' cells will truly revolutionise the treatment of life-threatening illnesses.

It is unclear at exactly what point the phrase "stem cell" entered the vernacular, one of very few scientific terms that achieve the status of, say, DNA in not requiring a detailed explanation every time it is written down or spoken.

Whether or not you know exactly what they are or what they do, stem cells imply something very specific: in them is invested the next generation of medicine, revolutionary treatments for everything from Parkinson's to Alzheimer's. On the horizon, there is also the hope of growing genetically matched tissue (even whole organs) to replace anything that has been damaged by disease or accident.

But perhaps the reason stem cells managed to lodge themselves so deep in the public psyche was not just because of their awesome scientific potential, or their ability to turn into the treatments of the future. Perhaps it was politics. For years, stem cells dominated all other science stories in newspaper headlines because they framed an ethical conundrum – to get to the most versatile stem cells meant destroying human embryos.

---

6 **the vernacular** [vəˈnækjələ] everyday or ordinary speech – 16 **psyche** [ˈsaɪki:] mind, spirit – 20 **conundrum** [kəˈnʌndrəm] challenging problem to solve – 22 **political football** *(idm)* sth controversial; a topic that is discussed in politics often

Research on stem cells became a political football, leading to delays in funding for scientists, particularly in the US. Not that the work itself was straightforward – the process of extracting stem cells from embryos is difficult and there is a very limited supply of material. Inevitable disappointment followed the years of headlines – where were the promised treatments? Was it all over-hyped?

For Paul Fairchild, co-director of the newly founded Oxford Stem Cell Institute, disappointment is just not on the agenda. Over a coffee in the University of Oxford's pathology department, where he is a professor, he explains his vision for the coming, post-hype decade of stem cell science.

"It's an exciting time in stem cell biology for a host of reasons," he says. "We've entered a whole new phase in the stem cell field, which has been held up enormously by ethical issues for over a decade."

Key to this is the discovery, in the past few years, of a way to make stem cells that do not require the destruction of embryos. In one move, these induced pluripotent stem (iPS) cells remove the ethical roadblocks faced by embryonic stem cells and, because they are so much easier to make, give scientists an inexhaustible supply of material, bringing them ever closer to those hoped-for treatments.

Fairchild says that iPS technology will "completely revolutionise the whole of medicine this century". And the talk is matched by action: the Oxford Stem Cell Institute is a recognition of the importance of the work ahead, a collaboration that brings together 37 laboratories across 17 departments at the university. "It's an attempt to try and bring all of the work in stem cell biology under one umbrella organisation to allow people to collaborate more effectively."

---

12 **a host of** *here:* myriad or many – 14 **to hold up** to delay – 18 **to induce** create or bring about – 18 **pluripotent** ability to create different types of cells – 19 **roadblock** obstacle *(Hindernis)* – 20 **inexhaustible** unending

Stem cells are the body's master cells, the raw material from which we are built. Unlike normal body cells, they can reproduce an indefinite number of times and, when prodded in the right way, can turn themselves into any type of cell in the body. The most versatile stem cells are those found in the embryo at just a few days old – this ball of a few dozen embryonic stem (ES) cells eventually goes on to form everything that makes up a person.

In 1998, James Thomson at the University of Wisconsin-Madison announced that he had isolated human ES cells in the lab. Finally, these powerful cells were within the grasp of scientists to experiment with, understand and develop into fixes for the things that go wrong.

There were some immediate practical problems with the work. Once scientists had extracted ES cells from an embryo, they could create an immortal line of the cells to use in research. But the wide genetic variations in humans mean that scientists need lots of different lines of ES cells to treat and understand the wide variety of faults. Each new line of ES cells can only be created by fertilising an egg, and these are a precious, rare commodity.

This is also where the ethical problems lie. Extracting ES cells destroys the embryo – for some, this is akin to killing a potential human life. George W Bush banned the use of federal dollars to support research using human ES cells on all but a limited number of cell lines that already existed in research labs prior to August 2001. Barack Obama reversed that ban, only to be thwarted by a federal court ruling in 2010 that, once again, put the scientists into a state of 🔗 uncertainty about stem cell research. By contrast, the

---

3 **prodded** stimulated – 5 **versatile** [ˈvɜrsət̬ᵊl] adaptable to many different functions – 9 **to isolate** separate or keep apart from others – 14 **to extract** remove with special effort or force – 15 **immortal** undying, eternal – 19 **commodity** [kəˈmɑːdət̬i] valuable item or resource – 21 **akin** [əˈkɪn] similar, equivalent – 25 **to thwart** [θwɔːrt] prevent sth from happening – 27 🔗 **For online link, use code fpcyxaw at klett-sprachen.de. For Klett Augmented, scan page 161.**

UK laws are relatively civil – after much debate about the ethics of using human embryos, the government passed strict, but fair, laws that allowed ES research to go ahead.

But that did not get rid of the practical problems of a lack of donor eggs, or that the experiments with ES cells as treatments – to repair a damaged heart, for instance – were proving unsuccessful.

Enter the iPS cell. In 2007, Shinya Yamanaka at Kyoto University in Japan demonstrated a way of producing ES-like cells without using eggs. He took a skin cell and, using a virus, inserted four specific bits of DNA into the skin cell's nucleus. The skin cell incorporated the genetic material and was regressed into an ES-like cell – it had been "reprogrammed" using a batch of chemicals in the lab. In a few short experiments, scientists had a near-limitless supply of stem cells that were, seemingly, as good as ES cells for their research.

By creating iPS cells from patients with genetic diseases, scientists have been able to watch which genes go wrong in a variety of conditions, how and when it happens – all of it critical detail in finding ways to stop diseases in their tracks.

The method works like this: take some skin cells from a person with Parkinson's disease and then regress these back into iPS cells. Then coax these stem cells to turn into neurons and watch how they work and, crucially, how they go wrong. These neurons are genetically identical to the patient's own brain cells – allowing scientists to model the disease more accurately and test out ideas or even screen potential drugs.

"It's possible now, of course, to take a few cells from an individual with an intractable disease of some kind for which there are no animal models or any way of studying it, to reprogramme them to

---

1 **civil** ['sivəl] generous, kind – 10 **nucleus** ['nu:kliəs] *Zellkern* – 11 **to regress** return to a previous state of being – 12 **batch** *(inf)* group, bunch – 22 **coax** [koʊks] convince, manipulate – 28 **intractable** uncontrollable or difficult to manage

an iPS cell state and then differentiate from those the cell type that's affected from the disease," says Fairchild. "We now have a way of taking them from that person and studying the cell type itself in vitro that will almost certainly have symptoms of the disease. It's possible to produce these models of human disease in vitro which we've never had access to before."

Models using iPS cells have proliferated in a few short years: they are now available for, among other things, motor neurone disease, juvenile diabetes and sickle cell anaemia.

"It's exciting to have models that we can now probe and find out what is actually going on for the first time," says Fairchild. Traditionally, scientists use animal models of disease in order to carry out experiments or test brand new drugs – but these models are not perfect. Using human cells taken from a patient with a human disease is a more promising way of gauging what might happen in people.

Fairchild has been examining how to use iPS cells to modulate the body's immune system. It is a route, he hopes, to less rejection when people get transplants of replacement tissue. The same techniques could even develop into a better way to treat cancer.

He started by differentiating embryonic stem cells into a key part of the body's immune system called dendritic cells. These cells continually sample proteins, called antigens, that sit on the surface of everything in the body. If they determine that the antigen comes from something potentially dangerous or foreign, they set the body's killer T-cells to go after the danger and destroy it. On the flip side, the dendritic cells can also dial down the ferocity of the killer T-cells if they recognise an antigen as non-foreign.

---

3 **in vitro** *(Lat)* done in a test tube or petri dish – 7 **proliferate** [proʊˈlɪfəreɪt] increase or multiply very quickly – 9 **anaemia** [əˈniːmiə] blood disorder, too few red cells – 15 **gauge** [geɪʤ] estimate, measure – 27 **to dial down** *here*: weaken – 27 **ferocity** [fəˈrɑːsəṱi] intensity

One way Fairchild's team is using this idea is to grow dendritic cells that can recognise the antigens on tumours. Inserting these cells into a patient would dial up the immune system's natural response to that tumour. "What you do is grow the dendritic cells, then feed them with the tumour-associated antigens in vitro," he says. "Then put those back into the patient, so that they're presenting those melanoma antigens."

His experiments have shown that the dendritic cells do indeed stimulate the body's T-cells to respond robustly. The T-cells are then programmed to find the tumour and destroy it. That means a better natural response to cancer, all without the need for toxic chemotherapy.

Another way to use the dendritic cells is to dial down the body's immune response to transplanted tissue or organs. Anyone who has a transplant needs immunosuppressant drugs for the rest of their lives to prevent their immune systems from attacking the new tissue. Stem cells offer the possibility of growing genetically matched tissue for patients, so rejection should, in theory, not be a problem.

But Fairchild points out that growing matched tissue for every individual is likely to be prohibitively expensive for now. Instead, scientists would probably grow replacements from a bank of stem cells that are close matches to the majority of the population. But that means that replacement tissue would still provoke the recipient's immune system.

Fairchild's solution is to grow dendritic cells from the same stem cells being used to grow the replacement tissue for the patient. The dendritic cells can then be used to train the recipient's immune system that the replacement tissue is not to be rejected.

The creativity in the field is exciting, but it is right, also, to point out the many technical issues facing iPS cells in moving outside the

7 **melanoma** tumor *usu* in skin cells – 15 **immunosuppressant** sth that prevents or stops natural response of body

lab. Just recently, Andras Nagy of Mount Sinai hospital and Timo Otonkoski at the University of Helsinki found genetic abnormalities when creating iPS cells. In a study published in *Nature*, they reported the deletion or amplification of certain strands of DNA. "Our analysis shows that these genetic changes are a result of the reprogramming process itself, which raises the concern that the resultant cell lines are mutant or defective," said Nagy.

It is just one of a number of research papers raising concerns about the way iPS cells are produced. "In a laboratory dish, pluripotent stem cells promise to become any sort of cell a researcher could want," wrote Monya Baker, editor of *Nature Reports Stem Cells*, in a 2009 article looking to the future of the iPS technology. "But when transplanted into the body, such cells could grow unpredictably: clinicians worry most about tumour formation, although one can imagine other dangers, such as tissues growing in the wrong place."

The very things that make iPS cells so useful in lab situations – their immortality and versatility – would be disastrous if left unchecked inside people. But, for a field that is barely a few years old, the remarkable pace of achievement should give plenty of hope that these challenges will be met. "Turning knowledge into medicine is never easy," says Baker. "But the pace of knowledge generation itself is fast and furious."

(1,939 words)

---

4 **deletion** eradication, destruction *(Vernichtung)* – 4 **amplification** [ˌæmplɪfɪˈkeɪʃᵊn] increase in number – 8 **to raise concerns** to make people aware of the problems – 18 **immortality** *Unsterblichkeit* – 18 **versatility** flexibility

Text 3: Article
Inside a Creepy Global Body Parts Business

By Martina Keller and Markus Grill, Der Spiegel, August 2009

The German company Tutogen's business in body parts is as secretive as it is lucrative. It extracts bones from corpses in Ukraine to manufacture medical products, as part of a global market worth billions that is centered in the United States.

Anatoly Korzhak, a pensioner and former engineer, died in Kiev on August 5, 2004. His body was picked up at 2 a.m. and taken to the forensic medicine institute in the Ukrainian capital. That same night, Korzhak's daughter, Lena Krat, received a telephone call and was asked to come to the institute as soon as possible the following morning, where she was told she would receive further information.

It was the first time Krat was confronted with the death of a close relative. "I was so upset that I couldn't think clearly," she recalls. When she arrived at the institute in the morning, a man there said something to her about skin transplants. He was an employee of a Ukrainian company that works hand-in-hand with forensic medicine experts. She said to the man: "Leave me alone. I don't understand what you're talking about, and I don't want to listen to you."

But the employee was persistent and eventually gave her a form to sign. He told her that if she consented to skin removal, she would be helping pediatric burn victims who needed transplants. Krat signed the form. "It was as if I had been hypnotized," she says.

---

2 **secretive** *(adj)* made into a secret *(geheimnisvoll)* – 3 **corpse** [kɔːrps] dead body – 8 **forensic** *kriminaltechnisch* – 23 **pediatric** [ˌpiːdiˈætrɪk] *adj* relating to medicine focused on children

But now Krat, a mother of two young girls, has learned from SPIEGEL that the Ukrainian company in question sends the body parts to a German company, Tutogen Medical GmbH, which in turn apparently supplies large numbers of such parts to the American tissue market.

In addition to strips of skin, tendons, bones and cartilage are removed from the bodies. "This shocks me," says Krat. "If I had known that so much is cut out, I would never have given my consent."

A Lucrative Industry

The incident in the Ukrainian capital is part of the secretive daily routine of a little-known but highly lucrative branch of the medical industry, in which companies use corpses to make medical spare parts. In doing so, they reuse almost everything the human body has to offer: bones, cartilage, tendons, muscle fascia, skin, corneas, pericardial sacs and heart valves. In the jargon of the profession, all of this is referred to as tissue.

Bones and tendons, the parts that interest Tutogen the most, are subjected to complex processing. The company degreases and cleans bones, cuts, saws or mills them into the desired shapes, then sterilizes, packages and sells the finished product in more than 40 countries around the world. With a prescription, it is even possible to order Tutogen's products through online pharmacies.

The market for tissue products is still small in Germany. When it comes to bones, for example, experts estimate that only about 30,000 transplants a year are used in hospitals nationwide, mainly

---

3 **in turn** after this – 6 **tendon** *Sehne* – 6 **cartilage** [ˈkɑːrt̬ᵊˈlɪʤ] *Knorpel* – 15 **fascia** [ˈfæʃiə] thin tissue around muscle – 16 **pericardial** [ˌperɪˈkɑːrdiᵊl] surrounding the heart and valves – 19 **to degrease sth** to remove the grease *(Fett)* from sth – 20 **to mill** to grind or crush *(usu:* into powder*)* – 22 **prescription** written order for medicine or medical products which a doctor makes for a patient *(Rezept)*

for use in bone reconstruction for hip surgery and in spinal column surgery.

It's a completely different story in the United States. According to the American Academy of Orthopedic Surgeons, more than a million bone parts are used in transplants every year. In no other country is it possible to make so much money with body parts. If a body were disassembled into its individual parts, then processed and sold, the total proceeds could amount to $ 250,000 (€ 220,000). For a single corpse! The US tissue industry generates total revenues of about $ 1 billion a year, says journalist Martina Keller, a co-author of this article and the author of the German book, "Cannibalized: The Human Corpse as a Resource."

Legal and Ethical Questions

This raises the question of just how legal the process of obtaining raw materials is. And are bone products made from corpses even medically necessary? According to Klaus-Peter Günther, president of the German Society of Orthopedics and Orthopedic Surgery, they are often "not the first choice" in operations. "For us, the gold standard is still tissue taken directly from the patient in question."

Alternatives are only an option, says Günther, when the material from the patient's body is insufficient. Those alternatives include animal bones and artificial replacement parts made of ceramic material, for example – or human donor bones.

Many hospitals collect and reuse bone fragments removed from patients who have received artificial hips. "For this reason," says Günther, "we have not had to resort to dead donors so far."

In the United States, doctors have fewer qualms about using body parts from corpses than their German counterparts – in such areas

1 **spinal column** *Wirbelsäule* – 4 **orthopedic** [ˌɔːrθoʊˈpiːdɪk] relating to the study or correction of bone and muscles – 21 **insufficient** not enough – 23 **donor** [ˈdoʊnɚ] **bones** bones which have been donated (given) voluntarily – 27 **qualm** [kwɑːm] problem or feeling of doubt

as spinal surgery, sports injuries and cosmetic surgery. For instance, doctors used pulverized skin particles to enhance lips and smooth out wrinkles.

Should corpses be butchered to make cosmetic procedures possible? Ingrid Schneider is against the practice. For the past 15 years the Hamburg political scientist, a former member of the Investigative Commission on Law and Ethics in Modern Medicine in the German parliament, has been involved in the subject of recycling body substances. Schneider argues that the body is not a source of raw materials that can be sold at will. Given such concerns, it is not surprising that many people are deeply opposed to allowing the body of a family member to be reused, even for medical purposes.

"Even if it is unrealistic to hope and fight for a total ban on the commercialization of the body in modern medicine," says Schneider, "it is important to set boundaries." For that reason, she insists that human tissue ought to be used sparingly – that is, only when such use is medically necessary and clearly superior to other forms of treatment.

The conviction that the body is much more than an object has also shaped the policies of the World Health Organization (WHO), the European Parliament and the European Council, the EU's body representing the leaders and ministers of the 27-member bloc. All of these institutions condemn the practice of trading in human body parts for profit.

In Germany, the country's organ transplant laws regulate the removal of tissue. Only those who have consented to organ and tissue harvesting are considered as donors. If a person dies and is not already a donor, his or her closest relatives can consent to

---

4 **to butcher** ['bʊtʃə˞] slaughter, cut into small pieces *(esp* as meat*)* – 10 **raw materials** *Rohstoffe* – 20 **conviction** [kən'vɪkʃᵊn] strong belief or opinion – 28 **harvesting** the collection and picking *(usu* of food*) das Ernten*

donation for them. But Paragraph 17 of the Transplant Act explicitly states: “Trading in organs or tissue intended for use in the medical treatment of others is prohibited.” And although the law does not prohibit physicians who remove tissue to be paid a suitable fee for their efforts, it does stipulate prison sentences of up to five years for anyone involved in the actual trading of body parts.

Part 2: A Booming Tissue Market

Tutogen paid its Ukrainian partners a fixed price for each body part. In January 2002, the company paid €42.90 for a complete femur, €42.90 for a humerus and €13.30 to €16.40 for a pericardial sac, depending on its size. Graduated prices were also arranged with the Ukrainians. Take, for example, the removal of patellar tendons with bone segments, known as “bond-tendon-bone,” or BTB. When coroners supplied less than 40 BTBs on-site, Tutogen paid €14.30 apiece. For larger numbers of BTBs, the price went up: to €23 apiece for 40 or more BTBs and to €26.10 for 60 or more. For a coroner, who makes about €200 ($287) a month in Ukraine, such graduated prices must have been an incentive to remove as much body material as possible.

Thousands of pages of internal memos, faxes, supply lists and documents from the years 2000 to 2004, which SPIEGEL has obtained, suggest that not only did Tutogen process the Ukrainian body parts itself, but it also supplied the US tissue market.

Florida-based RTI Biologics, one of the US market leaders in the industry, generated $147 million in sales in 2008. The company describes itself as the “leading provider of sterile biological implants for surgeries around the world.”

---

4 **fee** payment, reimbursement – 9 **femur** [ˈfiːmɚ] thigh bone – 10 **humerus** [ˈhjuːməras] upper arm bone – 12 **patellar tendons** kneecap tissue that connects muscles from upper to lower leg – 14 **coroner** official person who investigates cause of death

To that end, RTI acquired Tutogen Medical, Inc., the American parent company of the German company Tutogen Medical GmbH, last year. The acquisition was good news for RTI shareholders, because of Tutogen's large international donor network, says CEO Brian Hutchison. Put differently, Tutogen is a company that knows the ins and outs of gaining access to as many body parts as possible.

The body parts from Ukraine are shipped by air to Frankfurt or Nuremberg. From there, they are taken to the Tutogen headquarters in Neunkirchen am Brand, a town of 8,000 people in northern Bavaria.

Tutogen's facilities in Neunkirchen, just a few kilometers north of Nuremberg, comprise several low, warehouse-like buildings, where about 140 people work. All in all, it is an inconspicuous place for visitors who fly in regularly from Ukraine and the United States.

Company President Karl Koschatzky refused to respond to requests for an interview, and the company declined to answer a list of questions sent to its offices.

The Middleman

Tutogen uses a middleman to organize its deliveries from Ukraine. Dr. Igor Aleshenko, a coroner by training, manages the company's relationships with the various local forensic medicine institutes. He has been working for Tutogen in Ukraine for about 10 years.

In that time, Aleshenko has become a wealthy man, and he now divides his time between his two residences, one in Kiev and one in Moscow. In 2002, Tutogen described Aleshenko as a "cost-intensive person." He too was unavailable for an interview in Kiev, nor did he respond to written questions.

---

6 **the ins and outs** *(n, pl)* the details, the inside story – 14 **inconspicuous** not obvious; hidden *(unauffällig)* – 21 **middleman** agent, frontman

In Ukraine, Aleshenko is far more than just Tutogen's local contact. He is also the director of Bioimplant, a company that manages tissue removal. Because of its close ties to the Ukrainian Health Ministry, Bioimplant is practically immune to intrusive government inspections of bone shipments crossing the border.

Ukrainians are kept somewhat in the dark when it comes to Bioimplant's true business dealings. According to the company's website, its "primary activity" is the "production of bio-implants" for use in Ukrainian patients. But what does Bioimplant really do?

Kiev, on a summer's day in 2009. Anyone seeking to pay a visit to Bioimplant's headquarters would be inclined to head to the company's official address at Patrice Lumumba Street 4/6, an office building with a number of tenants – where Bioimplant doesn't even have its own mailbox.

A guard and a doorman greet visitors and send them to the fourth floor, where Bioimplant's offices are supposedly located. Room 305 is in a long hallway of closed doors. There is not even a sign to identify the room as being associated with Bioimplant. A young man in a pinstriped suit opens the door. He says that he hasn't been working for Bioimplant for very long, and that most of his work consists of photocopying.

According to the young man, the company leases three rooms in the office complex, but Dr. Aleshenko is not in today. Tutogen brochures and packets of sterilized corpse bones are stacked in the next room. Instead of the expected production facility, the offices are nothing but a distribution site.

Tutogen developed its business relationship with Aleshenko about 10 years ago. During a trip to Tutogen headquarters in the Bavarian countryside in November 2001, Aleshenko met with Koschatzky at the Bayerischer Hof Hotel in Erlangen, near Nuremberg. The minutes of the meeting contain a list of "new

---

4 **intrusive** unwanted or invasive – 31 **minutes** ['mɪnɪts] **of the meeting** written record of what is said and decided in a meeting

pathologies" working for Tutogen in the eastern Ukrainian cities of Dnipropetrovsk, Poltava and Zhytomyr.

Aleshenko had apparently brought along a wish list to the meeting, and his German business partners were eager to comply. According to the minutes, "TTG (Tutogen) agreed to provide 5,000 Deutschmarks for investment costs in Dnipropetrovsk (Ukraine). Dr. Aleshenko will send us the necessary payment instructions."

Unkosher Discussions

Some of the issues discussed at the meeting were less than kosher. For instance, the minutes state: "TTG is testing whether depilation of the corpse prior to skin removal could alleviate the hair problem (perhaps using the hot wax or cold wax method)."

A list of "pathologies currently providing (parts)," dated November 2001, already included abbreviations for 15 facilities in Ukraine. In the 2000–2001 fiscal year alone, 1,152 bodies in Ukraine were used to provide tissue for Tutogen.

But it still wasn't enough for the company, which needed more institutions to cooperate and more donors and more bone parts to supply a booming tissue market.

According to an internal planning document dated June 17, 2002 (the file is entitled "Raw Tissue Requirements"), Tutogen needed the following parts for the coming fiscal year:

- 2,920 shafts of the femur,
- 3,000 iliac crests,
- 1,190 patellar tendons,
- 3,750 kneecaps,
- 10,200 femoral muscle fascia (or fascia lata),
- 50 cranial bones,
- 70 Achilles tendons.

---

1 **pathology** study of body tissue and diseases – 10 **depilation** removal of all hair – 24 **iliac crests** [ˈɪliæk] upper wing part of pelvic bone

Aleshenko, whom Tutogen apparently paid directly for the tissue parts, is believed to have funneled part of the money to coroners in Dnipropetrovsk, Kiev, Kharkiv and other Ukrainian cities. According to an internal list of "paid incoming goods," Tutogen's Ukrainian partner received roughly €350,000 between January and August 2001.

The investment must have paid off. Online pharmacies charge between € 367 and € 854, depending on the size, for a Tutoplast Spongiosa Block (Bone Substance). According to the price lists used at the time, the Ukrainians received between € 23 and € 26.10 for the original body part, again depending on the size. Even if Tutogen were paying twice as much for the raw material today, it would still be a bargain.

Part 3: Tissue and Organ Harvesting

Not surprisingly, Tutogen could afford to be generous to its Ukrainian partners. That generosity included large quantities of equipment, which the company routinely sent on to its hardworking coroners.

According to the internal documents, in the 2000–2001 fiscal year Tutogen shipped 6,000 scalpels, 2,600 pairs of sterile gloves, 500 surgical gowns, 15 hacksaw blades for autopsies and many other items to Ukraine – at a total cost of € 40,000 in "donor expenses without tissue," as the Tutogen bookkeepers noted fastidiously. Tutogen paid its Ukrainian partners roughly € 500,000 for the body parts during the same period.

The US Food and Drug Administration (FDA) currently lists 20 facilities in Ukraine that are authorized to supply body parts for the US market. But no matter which of these facilities one clicks on in the FDA database, all share the same contact information: the

21 hacksaw blade *Handbügelsägeblatt; -klinge*

telephone number of Tutogen Medical GmbH in northern Bavaria.

One of the facilities on the list is the forensic medicine institute in Krivoy Rog, an industrial city in southeastern Ukraine, with a population of about 700,000. According to the FDA database, the Krivoy Rog site is authorized to supply bones, cartilage, fascia, ligaments, pericardial sacs, sclera (the white of the eye), skin and tendons.

Tissue and Organ Harvesting

The whitewashed, Spartan structure housing the forensic medicine institute is on the edge of the hospital grounds. Frosted glass windowpanes behind latticed windows discourage prying eyes. Visitors immediately notice the cloying odor of death upon entering the building. The director of the institute is unavailable, even though his car is parked on the hospital grounds. A doctor wearing a denim jacket assumes the task of getting rid of anyone inquiring about the institute's collaboration with the German company.

He tells us reporters to contact the district attorney's office and points to a sign above the door, which reads: "No Admittance without Authorization." We ask whether that includes Tutogen. "No, Tutogen is not unauthorized here," the man says, indicating that the conversation is over.

The former director of the city's forensic medicine department, Vladimir Bondarenko, is slightly more forthcoming. A retiree, he meets with visitors at a street café. "Tissue harvesting began at his department about 10 years ago," says Bondarenko.

"It was illegal," he says. "The relatives of the deceased should have been told about what was happening with the bodies, but they had

10 **Spartan** *here:* simple, plain – 12 **prying eyes** looking at sth even though doing so is secret and against the will of sb else – 13 **cloying odor** ['oʊdɚ] bad, old smell – 24 **forthcoming** *here:* talkative, ready to give information

no idea. When the deceased is lying in the coffin, the family members see nothing but the face. What they don't see is that the bones of the legs or arms have been removed."

The Ukrainian Tissue Transplant Act includes a provision stating that family members must consent to tissue donation if the deceased did not already do so while alive. However, there are indications that this was often not the case. Ukrainian authorities in Krivoy Rog and several other cities are conducting investigations into suspected illegal tissue and organ harvesting.

The case of the deceased father of Lena Krat, from Kiev, for example, was examined in connection with an investigation identified by the file number 50-3793, begun on January 1, 2005. The investigation covered the period between May and September 2004. The names of ten deceased persons are listed in the files. Their family members stated that they "did not consent to the removal of anatomical material."

According to the court order authorizing the proceedings, "family members were deceived, in that they were told that only a small part of the deceased would be removed, such as a bone or tissue fragment. In actual fact, almost all bones and tissue were removed. … All of the material was taken to Germany."

A Legal Twist

Despite the evidence, the Kiev district attorney's office closed the proceedings in July 2005, "in the absence of a statutory offense." Curiously, the document states that the reason why the case was dropped was that Bioimplant employees had not violated the transplant act, because they had not "transplanted" material from corpses, but had merely *removed* it so that it could be processed into

---

4 **provision** legal requirement – 15 **consent (to)** agree (to) – 24 **statutory offense** illegal action

"bio-implants." As a result of this legal loophole, the recycling of corpses has been allowed to continue to this day.

Back in Kiev, the forensic medicine institute on Orangery Street is a long, brick building, from which doctors wearing light-green aprons occasionally emerge to smoke cigarettes outside the front door. Family members stand next to the entrance, waiting for the release of their dead relatives. There is a display of coffins and wreaths in front of a funeral parlor across the street.

Vladimir Yurchenko is the director of the institute. He points to the room where bodies are processed for Tutogen. It is on the ground floor and closed to outsiders. Why? "Because that's what the US health authorities require," says Yurchenko.

Kiev's senior forensic pathologist explains the process. Bioimplant obtains the relatives' consent, and company employees also come to the institute to harvest the body parts. Yurchenko's staff members assist in the process, for which they receive additional compensation. Once bones and other parts have been removed, wooden sticks are inserted into the body so that it retains its shape until the funeral.

The harvested bones, tendons and pieces of cartilage are stored in zinc-plated metal boxes in a refrigerated room in the basement. "The tissue parts are brought up once every few weeks, when a truck comes and takes them away," says Yurchenko. Karl Koschatzky, the secretive Tutogen executive from Bavaria, also turns up occasionally.

Part 4: 'A Source of Raw Materials'

According to Yurchenko, about 8,000 corpses a year are delivered to the forensic medicine department. Of that number, more than 5,000 are potential bone donors, but family members only consent to

---

5 **apron** *Schürze* – 8 **wreath** [ri:θ] decorative arrangement of flowers or leaves *usu* at a funeral

harvesting from about 150 bodies. If the two facilities in the capital already provide parts from about 150 bodies each, as Yurchenko says, and if a total of 20 facilities in Ukraine are registered with the FDA – and, therefore, are collaborating with Tutogen – it can be assumed that the German company obtains its body parts from large numbers of Ukrainian corpses. "All we are for the rich countries is a source of raw materials," says Yurchenko.

In May 2004, Tutogen signed a five-year contract with Bioimplant, which describes the process as follows: "The Ukrainians transfer harvested tissue to Tutogen in Germany to have it processed into products." But this processing is costly. How does the Ukrainian company pay for the expensive processing? The answer is very simple: with the bones from Ukrainian corpses that have been processed into products in Germany. This is the currency accepted by both parties to the arrangement.

What the agreement does not state is that the Germans were not producing products for Bioimplant, but were ordering substantial amounts of raw material from the Ukrainians every month.

At times, much larger numbers of body parts from Ukraine and other countries were arriving in Neunkirchen than Tutogen could even process. A document titled "Inventory, Raw Material Storage 1," dated March 2000, reveals the scope of this excess material. According to this inventory document, Tutogen warehouses already contained 688 patellar tendons, 1,831 kneecaps, 1,848 fibula, 2,114 fascia and 1,196 foot bones, or a total of more than 20,000 body parts.

In June 2002, Tutogen employees wrote the following comments in the minutes of a meeting: "Warehouse problems. More tissue than necessary continues to be delivered. Solutions are needed to address this problem."

---

22 **scope** extent, amount *(Ausmaß)*

The company documents also include references to the kinds of solutions Tutogen had in mind. According to an internal memo dated April 2002, a Ms. R. noted "… that there is no longer any storage capacity in the deep freezers. Efforts must be stepped up to ship tissue to the USA."

According to a document dated June 2002, which lists the "Raw Tissue Requirements for USA Needs," the US partners required the following monthly supply:

- 119 iliac crests,
- 667 pieces of fascia lata,
- 267 kneecaps,
- 243 shafts of the femur.

Did Tutogen Break the Law?

Apparently, the deliveries to the United States were not only sent to the parent company in Florida, Tutogen Medical Inc., which could have been explained as a way of shifting the problem within the company, but also to RTI, the company's US competitor at the time.

In a table detailing a shipment from Lugansk in Ukraine, delivered on Dec. 7, 2001, a sum of €62,000 is quoted, but the recipient is identified as "TM/RTI."

If Tutogen was indeed shipping unprocessed tissue to the United States, this could constitute participation in the illegal tissue trade, provided a profit was generated as a result.

In an internal memo dated April 4, 2002, a Tutogen employee wrote the following cautioning statement: "We should avoid shipping unprocessed raw material to TMUS (Tutogen USA), so as not to create the impression of participating in the tissue trade."

---

16 **to shift** to move (temporarily) – 23 **to constitute** to mean, to be the same as, to amount to – 26 **cautioning** ['kɑːʃənɪŋ] asking (sb) to be careful, warning sb

The German Institute for Cell and Tissue Replacement, another major bone producer, categorically rejects such practices. Director Hans-Joachim Mönig insists that "obtaining raw tissue from one country and passing it on to third parties is against the law. In our view, this constitutes the crime of trading in tissue."

To date, its collaboration with Aleshenko and the Kiev Health Ministry has worked exceedingly well for Tutogen. All investigations against Tutogen's Ukrainian partners in Krivoy Rog, Kiev and Dnipropetrovsk have been suspended.

But that could change. Last year, the public prosecutor's office in Krivoy Rog launched a new investigation.

Once again, forensic medicine employees, as the public prosecutor's office states in response to SPIEGEL's inquiry, are suspected of "having used coercion and fraud to obtain the consent of family members for the removal of tissue and other anatomical material for purposes of transplantation." Seventeen family members of the deceased have already testified.

On Jan 9, 2009, the district attorney's office submitted the case to the relevant district court, where the case is still underway.

Lena Krat, the Kiev woman who was persuaded to release her father's body for tissue harvesting in 2004, wants those responsible to be finally brought to justice. "Those people are truly guilty," she says, "and I am outraged that these terrible things are still taking place."

(3,940 words)

---

6 **to date** *(adv)* up until now – 10 **public prosecutor** lawyer who leads the case for the state against an accused person or people – 14 **coercion** [ˌkoʊˈɜːrʃᵊn] trying to force sb to do sth they do not want to do – 14 **fraud** [frɑːd] deception, scam, trickery – 18 **district attorney** public official representing state government in court

Make notes here on what this section has contributed to your bigger picture of "Visions of the Future".

Now you have read all the texts, make notes here on your bigger picture of "Visions of the Future"